Drug
Names
Decoded

Tony Guerra, Pharm.D.

Drug Names Decoded

2nd Edition

ISBN: 978-1-300-10210-6

To Mindy
Brielle, Rianne and Teagan

Foreword

In the fall of 1994, I went to my first week long experience in a pharmacy as a pharmacy student. At this grocery chain, the pharmacy manager was in charge of anything that was not food, so he was in charge of all the over-the-counter medications. After a brief introduction, he said I should come out and spend time learning the drugs out here. *I had no idea how.*

Academically, I should have been able to. At that time I had completed Calculus I and II, Inorganic and Organic Chemistry I and II, Biology I and II, Physics I and II, and a course in Biochemistry, yet I had no idea how to break up such a big project, learning the drugs, and turn it into a manageable series of steps. Eventually, over four years that included 2,000 hours in a pharmacy as an intern and another 2,000 hours working as a pharmacy technician, I eventually learned the drug names. Now, as someone who teaches pharmacology, I realize it doesn't need to take that long if we look at the process differently.

Instead of first learning pharmacology as a science alone, it is better to approach pharm (the abbreviation students use) as a language to be learned. Just as you would go into another country and learn food words in a restaurant by looking at the menu, the pharmacy aisles are set up so you can learn different classes of medication by their own menu of choices. This book is set up so you can go into the aisles and pick up some of the language by just looking at the shelves and noticing words in a different way.

Someone does not need to have had all those science classes to learn drug names very quickly if they know what to look for and in what order to look for it. This is a good thing, because many students who want to be in health care (pre-medicine, pre-nursing, pre-pharmacy, pre-dental, pre-physical therapy, and so forth) can take a big step forward with just a small time commitment and some odd looks from the staff at their local pharmacy.

If I had had a field guide, with space left for notes, then I would have had exactly what I needed to leave that pharmacy with working knowledge of the drug names. I could make learning a lifelong; rather, than compartmentalized process.

Putting myself in my students' shoes

My pharmacology students struggled with the correct pronunciation and memorization of drug names. Because I had been pronouncing them for so long, I didn't realize I had "learned the language" and I couldn't see how to best help students get around the challenge. I took a week to try to learn French, a language I didn't know. Immediately, I understood the three major challenges:

1. It's tough to learn and memorize a word if you can't pronounce it. Most French words use the same Roman "A to Z" alphabet as English, but the pronunciations are very different or unfamiliar just like generic drug names.

2. In the pharmacology books I used, I found many generic names in the first chapters. Those generic names are in the language of organic and biochemistry, a class that most of my students had not taken. In contrast, the language books always define a word immediately before or after introducing it so nothing is unfamiliar.

3. Finally, I found clues in the brand names of the drugs that hinted what they were for, as I found French words that had remnants of English words (cognates and false-cognates) that I already knew.

After opening myself up to language as a key to learning pharmacology, I moved from the pursuit of learning French to learning Latin. Latin has a myriad of suffixes and strange endings and cannot be readily translated word for word. I now felt like a student again: frustrated, lost and pounding my head asking myself, "Why don't I get this?" In addition, my triplet daughters were born taking away a significant amount of my time. I could only learn in small, often interrupted bites.

Eventually, I accepted two facts: 1. I needed to get help from other people to learn a new language efficiently. 2. These people, on YouTube at least, were writing poems and songs. A song helped me learn the six endings for the present indicative:

Person/Number	English Verb	Latin Verb
I	Love	Amo
You	Love	Amas
He, She, It	Loves	Amat
We	Love	Amamus
You all	Love	Amatis
They	Love	Amant

Similar to pharmacology, the stem of the word love ama- stays the same similar to how the suffixes or prefixes often stay the same for pharmacologic drugs. After this realization I made up the *Cardiode to Joy* which goes to the beat of Beethoven's *Ode to Joy* which is found in the cardiology chapter of this book. Memorizing words alone will not get you there. It is with a combination of sentences, stories, poetry, prose and song that can make pharmacology a favorite subject.

You will start seeing pharmacologic challenges to be solved in television shows, commercials and movies. The anxiety riddled Bob in "What about Bob?" The "Gas man" hit-man from "Dumb and Dumber" suffers from an ulcer. There is a Parkinsonian tremor in "Awakenings" and the use of the drug L-Dopa. You can find examples in Emily Dickinson's "I Felt a Funeral in my Brain" for headache, Edgar Allan Poe's "Tell Tale Heart" for hypertension, the "Dialogue between Ben Franklin and Gout" for gout, "The Love Song of J. Alfred Prufrock" by T.S. Eliot for social anxiety disorder, Kate Chopin's "The Story of an Hour" for congestive heart failure, and so forth.

Hopefully, each time you come across an instance, you write it in this book, to further connect the drug's use to your memory.

Contents

INTRODUCTION – THE LANGUAGE OF PHARMACOLOGY

Professional school campus-gatherings were usually referred to by the type of student that was expected, i.e. a medical, nursing, law, or pharmacy student party. Generally, unaffiliated spouses and significant others felt very uncomfortable at these get-togethers, not because the people weren't friendly, but because they did not understand the language. My wife and I are both pharmacists, so when she talks about her problems at work, I understand both personally and professionally what she's talking about. This book approaches pharmacology in a way that you would feel comfortable, after reading it and completing the activities, in an arena with other health professionals with regard to medications.

Most pharmacology books come from one of two perspectives. Either it is expected that a student will have completed six semesters of study of inorganic, organic, and biochemistry (as in pharmacy school) or the student will have completed a study of anatomy, physiology, psychology, microbiology, and pathophysiology (as in nursing school) before starting their pharmacology coursework.

This book provides an alternate learning channel. I teach in a pharmacy technician program at a community college where students are simultaneously learning anatomy, medical terminology and pharmacology. In this case, a different route works better, and that is one of studying pharmacology from a language perspective.

Start with your own name

Tony – My first name translates into two easy to pronounce one-syllable English words, toe and knee.

Guerra – Cannot be pronounced with spoken English. I tell people it's pronounced like Sara with a G, but in reality there is an *erre* sound of rolling r's that is not found in spoken English.

The most famous last name in pronunciation is Boiardi, but he, Ettore Boiardi, chose to put the phonetic "Boyardee" on his Italian food so it would be pronounced correctly.

Think of brand names as first names, generic names as *Foreign Language* **last names**

The brand name is generally a two-to-three syllable nickname that *hints* at the drug's function, but by law, may not make a claim. The names are very much like a nickname such as Betsy or Jack. But a non-native English speaker would have no idea that Betsy comes from Elizabeth or Jack comes from Jonathan. The same is true with generic names. They are often unpronounceable because the sounds that form them are regularly used by *organic chemists* and *biochemists* and the brand names are distant relations to them.

For example, how would one know that Tylenol and acetaminophen are related as brand and generic name without seeing the actual full chemical name N-ace<u>ty</u>l-para-amino<u>phenol</u>? Or could one know that the brand-name drug Lopressor, which **lo**wers blood **press**ure, is metoprolol?

To get to know these drugs, it's easier to group them by their class and first names, eliciting something about them, then going on to learn the longer last names, the generics, which may have some commonalities in their prefixes and suffixes.

When you are learning a new language, it is best to start with the smaller words and work up. Also, it is nice to work with *cognates* or words that are similar to something you already know. In the case of this book, we'll first focus on drugs that are available over-the-counter, that a person can take this book and walk up to and see on a pharmacy shelf. Then, we'll move on to the drugs that are less accessible and by prescription only. Again, all of this is dictated by using a language, rather than scientific lens of study. As mentioned before:

Brand name: Often gives clue to function

The brand name, two to three syllables, often created by a marketing firm, will sometimes hint at the *function* of a drug, i.e. Lopressor creates **lo**wered blood **press**ure

Generic name: can help group different drugs

Lopressor's four syllable generic name, metoprolol, has a suffix of –olol which hints at the *drug class*, i.e. drugs that end in –olol are beta-blockers.

The importance of being able to *picture* words

Read this sentence aloud.

Jack walks to the pharmacy

When a student hears this they can picture a man, the action of walking and a building that is a pharmacy.

But, what about this sentence?

Jack gallivants to the pharmacy.

A student may not know the word "gallivant" means to wander. However, because Jack and pharmacy are at opposite ends of the sentence, a student may ignore the word.

Jack gallivants to the pharmacy.

The student correctly assumes Jack is going to the pharmacy and the mode of ambulating is irrelevant.

What happens if in this sentence the name is changed to something gender-neutral?

Pat gallivants to the pharmacy.

Now we have a name that can be short for Patricia or Patrick and a student can picture a person, not necessarily a gender possibly moving in some way to a pharmacy, clouding the meaning.

Finally the sentence might read.

Pat gallivants to the apothecary.

A student might not know that apothecary is a synonym for pharmacy. And to have a gender neutral person doing something somewhere creates a clouded understanding of what is happening. However, if the student asks for clarification about Pat's full name and looks up the definition of "gallivant" and "apothecary", the sentence becomes clear.

The same progression of difficulty can be true in a sentence involving pharmacology.

Read this sentence aloud.

Aspirin reduces fever.

Most people will have taken or come in contact with *aspirin*, an over-the-counter medication, they will understand that to *reduce* means to lower and they have seen or had a *fever* themselves. *In the person's mind three pictures might emerge.*

Bottle of aspirin // Down arrow // Person sweating with fever

The subject of the sentence can be changed in this way.

Celecoxib reduces fever.

A student can look up celecoxib, learn that it is a prescription non-steroidal anti-inflammatory drug (NSAID) in the same class as aspirin. By connecting that knowledge the student can know that a drug similar to aspirin and reduces fever. However, there is an added level of difficulty. How does someone pronounce celecoxib? What does celecoxib look like?

Pronunciation

Pronunciation is usually learned from hearing other people say the word, but when a student studies alone, they will need to either find a resource that pronounces it for them or ask someone who knows how. Most students, however, will not know they are pronouncing something wrong and will pronounce it as best they can.

Celecoxib is pronounced:

Cell (as in a jail cell)

Eh (How was dinner? Eh, it wasn't that good.)

Cox (cocks as in preparing a pistol to fire)

Ib (as in the last sound of the word fib)

Image

Googling celecoxib turns up images of the chemical compound and various capsules providing a visual of the drug.

The verb in the sentence might be changed in this way.

Celecoxib mitigates fever.

A student may not know that "mitigate" and "reduce" are synonyms and would need to look it up.

The direct object might be changed as well.

Celecoxib mitigates pyrexia.

A student may not know that "pyrexia" and "fever" are synonyms and would also need to look this up.

After these additional steps the student can now picture:

Bottle of celecoxib // Down arrow // Person sweating – fever

Why are the drugs so hard to pronounce?

Drug names elude students because the words contain the same 26 letters used in the English alphabet, but the syllables read like a foreign language.

In studying another language, usually there are many parts of speech to learn. In pharmacology only two parts of speech meet the reader: nouns or adjectives describing nouns in a noun phrase.

For example:

Ibuprofen (Motrin) is neither a person nor a place, but a thing, a noun.

Ibuprofen + tablet forms a noun phrase, where ibuprofen acts as an adjective describing the tablet.

That's it. No adverbs, verbs, pronouns, prepositions, conjunctions, or interjections.

How is a drug name formed?

With each drug, there are three types of names.

1) The chemical name

First, there is the most complex name, the IUPAC (International Union of Pure and Applied Chemistry) standard name, which makes perfect sense to a chemist.

(RS)-2-(4-(2-methylpropyl)phenyl)propanoic acid.

Second, there is an older way a chemist named compounds – the common name.

Iso-butyl-propanoic-**phen**olic acid which becomes I bu pro phen, **ibuprofen**, the generic name.

2) The Generic Name

While this transformation to ibuprofen is an improvement, it has four syllables. Drug companies prefer to use nicknames that have two to three syllables. However, the nicknames are likely to be unrelated to the generic name as mentioned earlier with Betsy and Elizabeth or Jack and Jonathan.

3) The brand/trade name

Two brand names for ibuprofen include Advil and Motrin, both with two easy-to-pronounce syllables.

Often the drug companies use *plosives* to make powerful stops in the word to make it memorable.

Say each of the following letters and see if you can feel it in your tongue or nose.

Tongue blade occlusion t or d

Tongue body occlusion k or g

Lip occlusion b or p

Nasal stops such as m or n

Motrin contains m, a nasal stop; t, a tongue blade occlusion; and n, another nasal stop. This forces the person saying the word to stop their breath three times, slowing the pronunciation of the word and keeping it on the tongue and/or nose longer.

Using mnemonics in pharmacology

Homophones

In grade school you may have learned the word "homophone" which is a word that may be spelled differently but sound the same.

Some examples include the words "there" and "their," "two" and "too," and "hear" and "here"

To remember which meaning should be associated with the correct word, the teacher may have told you to look inside the word for a clue:

In the word "their" you find "heir," such as the person who will inherit something. Then you can associate that the word "their" has to do with the possessive of a group of people versus "there" which means "in that place."

In the word "two" you can turn the w sideways to make a 3, spelling "t3o" so you can remember that two has to do with a number. Also, too has two o's, and you can remember that it has too many o's.

In the word "hear" you can find the word "ear" and you can remember that this form means to listen versus "here" which means "in this place."

Those clues are called **mnemonic** devices, something to help your memory. They also work in the memorization of the compound's names.

Pharmacology mnemonics with the brand name

Prilosec contains "Pr" which can be short for "proton" (H^+), the associated ion with something acidic.

Prilosec contains "lo" which can be short for "low."

Prilosec contains "sec" which can be short for "secretion."

Prilosec's mechanism of action is to inhibit proton pumps and reduce the acid in a person's stomach. By looking at the name of the drug we can see that "proton" "low" "secretion" also means a reduction in protons, helping us remember the meaning of the word.

Another more obvious brand name in the same class of drugs is **Prevacid which** contains "prev" which can be short for "prevent" and the word "acid." Prevacid prevents acid.

In the same light **Protonix** can be broken down into "proton" and "nix." To nix is a noun meaning "no" so "proton" "nix" mean "protons" "no" or "no protons."

Aciphex can be looked at as containing "aci," short for "acid," and "iphex" sounds like "affects," so this would combine to make "affects acid" or affects pH, a measure of acidity.

Pharmacology mnemonics with the generic name

The generic names of proton pump inhibitors contain a similar suffix, thus "-prazole" might be used to identify proton pump inhibitors as a class. By looking at the other drugs, we see this is the case.

Omeprazole (Prilosec)

Esomeprazole (Nexium)

Lansoprazole (Prevacid)

Dexlansoprazole (Kapidex)

Pantoprazole (Protonix)

Rabeprazole (Aciphex)

If you look carefully, you see that there is an es**omeprazole** and an **omeprazole** and a dex**lansoprazole** and **lansoprazole**.

Drugs with the same root word

Esomeprazole (Nexium)

In chemistry, compounds may have a mirror image, but instead of calling them right-handed and left-handed, we call them R and S from the Latin words *rectus* (right) and *sinister* (left). One is more active chemically in the body and that is usually the S form.

However, putting an "s" in front of omeprazole makes someprazole which would be pronounced "some" "prazole". Instead, the full syllable "es" allows for a separation between the S- and the compound, as a chemist would pronounce it.

Dexlansoprazole (Kapidex)

In chemistry, compounds also direct plane-polarized light either to the left or right. These terms are either "d" or "+" for dextrorotatory compounds rotating plane-polarized light to the right or "l" or "+-" designating levorotatory compounds rotating plane-polarized light to the left. Thus, the dexlansoprazole would be expected to rotate plane-polarized light to the right.

In both cases it is expected that the es- or dex- is a more effective form of the medication. This is sometimes the case, but not always. Often, by adding this new form a drug company can patent a new drug earning brand-name prices rather than generic prices for their compounds.

Other examples include the SSRI antidepressants:

Citalopram (Celexa)

Escitalopram (Lexapro)

And the stimulant medications:

Methylphenidate (Ritalin)

Dexmethylphenidate (Focalin)

Pharmacopoetry: Poetic feet in classical meter

Poetry used to be taught to help learn *rhetoric*, or improving a speaker's ability to perform. In pharmacology it can be invaluable in helping students say the drug names better.

U = unaccented
/ = accented

The accented, unaccented form /U is called a **trochee** such as **Mo**-trin, **Pro**-zac, or **Zo**-loft. Even my name is a combination of two trochees: **Toe**-Knee (Tony) **Gwhere**-uh (Guerra)

U/ is an **iamb** such as a-**leve** where the accent follows the unstressed syllable.

/ U U is a **dactyl** with three syllables, one accented, then two unaccented like **Lip**-i-tor.

U / U is an **amphibrach** which has three syllables, two unaccented with a central accent like Lan –**ox** – in.

The poetic meter (trochee, iamb, dactyl, amphibrach) is not as important as recognizing that a drug name has a place where the *stress* belongs. Almost all brand name drugs have an easy-to-digest two or three syllables in one of these poetic forms.

Common mistakes to avoid

Some common pronunciation mistakes come from trying to force a four-syllable-word into a more comfortable three syllables.

For example:

Atenolol, "uh-TEN-uh-lawl," is cut to atenol "at-EN-all"

Or

Simvastatin, "SIM-va-stat-in," is cut to simvastin "SIM-vas-tin"

Or

Sometimes a letter (r to t) is replaced:

A gene<u>r</u>ic drug becomes a gene<u>t</u>ic drug.

Or a letter (n) is omitted to make a known word:

Oxyco<u>n</u>tin "ox-e-CON-tin" is cut to oxy*cotton* "ox-e-COT-tin"

Or a sound is changed:

Metoprolol "meh-TOE-pruh-lawl" becomes "Met-UH-pro-lawl"

These mispronunciations take credibility away from a health practitioner.

Drug listing by physiologic system

Most books will list drugs by drug class, give a generic equivalent, and then a brand name in a chart or a list, from left to right. But a student who cannot pronounce the drugs will have difficulty; therefore it is better to go from right to left, learning a brand name first, generic second and, drug class last.

1. **The brand names**, with an expert team of marketers behind them, should be learned first by looking for clues as to their function with proper pronunciation.

2. Then, after learning the two to three syllable brand name, a student can look at **the generic name** and work to split it into manageable one to three syllable pieces. For example, hydrochlorothiazide's 7 syllables are better broken into hydro/chloro/thiazide when learning the name for the first time.

Also, the value of the suffixes and prefixes are not just about identifying the drug. By cutting the affix from the rest of the word, it reveals a very easily pronounced word. For example, ranitidine, famotidine, nizatidine, and cimetidine are all four-syllable words that are H_2 blockers. But when one takes the two syllable suffix –tidine away, what's left are the two-syllable fragments rani-, famo-, niza- and cime-. Now, instead of one difficult four-syllable word, there are two-manageable two-syllable fragments.

3. Finally, the student can look on the drugstore shelf or go on a pharmacy website like Walgreens.com or CVS.com to get pictures and additional information. This is especially important for *kinesthetic* learners, those students who *learn by doing*.

Start in the GI aisle, read the mnemonics, and write what you notice or what first comes to mind: Maybe it's a jingle, maybe it's a flavor, maybe it's where you were when you felt sick, but once you attach the experience you will learn the drug.

Drug categories

What confuses many students is how drug classes are named. Some drugs are named:

- **By what they do for the patient, also called the therapeutic class:** Anti-depressant
- **By their chemical structure:** Tricyclic antidepressants (TCA) (three rings in the compound)
- **By the receptor they affect:** Beta-blockers
- **By the neurotransmitter they affect:** Selective serotonin reuptake inhibitor (SSRI)

First, it comes down to creating two-and-three syllable words or manageable acronyms (letters to stand for a word). Anything longer is uncomfortable to say. Here is a sample dialogue:

What kind of anti-anxiety drug did the doctor put you on?

A *benzo*. (short for *benzodiazepine* [six syllables])

Did she give you anything for the depression?

Yes, an *SSRI*. (short for *selective serotonin reuptake inhibitor* [14 syllables])

And something for sleep?

Yes, a TCA. (short for *tricyclic antidepressant* [eight syllables])

Is that going to interfere with your heart medication?

You mean the *beta-blocker*? (short for beta-adrenergic-receptor-antagonist [13 syllables])

Or your cholesterol medication?

The *statin*? (the suffix of a class of drugs called the HMG-CoA reductase inhibitors, which itself is short for 3-hydroxy-3-methylglutaryl-Co-enzyme-A [21 syllables])

In that conversation, 15 syllables were used instead of 62.

However, most patients would not speak that clinically about the medications to each other; rather, patients speak to each other in common therapeutic class names (an SSRI becomes an anti-depressant, a beta-blocker becomes a pressure pill, a diuretic becomes a water pill, an HMG-CoA reductase inhibitor becomes a cholesterol pill) because from the patient's point of view, they only have one anti-depressant, one blood pressure pill, one water pill, and one cholesterol pill.

However, healthcare professionals must speak to each other in terms of chemical structure, receptors, and neurotransmitters because the patient is one of many and the specific type of pill carries specific adverse effects of which the practitioner must be aware and make the patient aware.

Learning these classes comes from using suffixes, prefixes, and just being around a healthcare environment. It's the lingo and it comes with time.

Pronunciation

I could have written the phonetic pronunciations for the drugs, however, I have found that it's easier for a student to digest small words, familiar sounds, and proper names. For example:

TYLENOL comes from the chemical name N-ac**tyl**-para-amino-ph**enol** (APAP).
"TIE-Len-all"

TIE is the accented syllable/**Len** is short for Lenny/ **all** is a synonym for everything.

ALL CAPS = accented syllable

Len = a capitalized proper name

A note about the brand name mnemonics:

I didn't call anyone at any brand name drug companies. I just looked at each drug name and used my experience as a teacher of pathophysiology, pharmacology, and organic and biochemistry and made up something that seemed to makes sense, but more importantly will help the student remember the drug's drug class or function. The FDA does not allow a drug company to name a drug after its intended use.

Chemistry students have it easier

Some students have organic and/or biochemistry in their background and many of the word parts are familiar to them from their own study. Unlike a medical terminology course where each stem, root, linking vowel, prefix, or suffix adds to the meaning of the word, often the chemical word parts have no relation to drug function. This is why drug development is a long trial-and-error-filled process that can cost up to a billion dollars for each viable drug. Here are some pronunciations of common organic chemistry terms.

Pronouncing word parts from organic chemistry

These words indicate the number of carbon atoms in an attached molecule made up only of carbon and hydrogen:

1. **Methyl** – *Methyl*phenidate
   "METH-ill"

2. **Ethyl** – Fentan*yl*
   "ETH-ill"

3. **Propyl** – Meto*pro*lol
   "PROP-ill"

4. **Butyl** – Al*but*erol
   "BYOOT-ill"

Levo and dextro mean left and right respectively:

- **Levo** - *Levo*thyroxine
  "LEE-vo"
- **Dextro** - *Dex*methyphenidate
  "DEX-trow"

These words mean there is a specific element in each molecule:

- **Thio** (sulfur) – Hydrochloro*thi*azide
  "THIGH-oh"
- **Chloro** (chlorine) – Hydro*chloro*thiazide
  "KLOR-oh"
- **Hydro** (hydrogen) – *Hydro*codone/APAP
  "HIGH-droe"

These words are branches that generally attach to the central molecule:

- **Acetyl** – Levetir*acet*am   "Uh-SEAT-ill"
- **Alcohol** – Tramad*ol*   "AL-kuh-haul"
- **Amide** – Loper*amide*   "UH-myde"
- **Amine** – Diphenhydr*amine*   "UH-mean"
- **Disulfide** – *Disulf*iram   "DIE-sulf-eyed"
- **Furan** – *Fur*osemide   "FYOOR-an"
- **Guanidine** – Cimet*idine*   "GWAN-eh-dean"
- **Hydroxide** – Magnesium *Hydroxide* "HI-drox-eyed"
- **Imidazole** – Omepr*azole*   "im-id-AZ-ole"
- **Ketone** – Spironolact*one*   "KEY-tone"
- **Phenol** – Acetamino*phen*   "FEN-ole"
- **Sulfa** – *Sulfa*methoxyzole   "SULL-fuh"

The poetry, songs and mnemonics.

The poems and songs found in this work are all ones I've written. I think it is valuable for you to write your own poems, songs and/or mnemonics because it will be more meaningful to you. This book has many examples that can help you. Students shy away from poetry because it's not cool, or it is perceived as difficult. However, I define poetry in this way:

Poem: Poetry

Take
a
picture

with
a
pencil

That's what you are working toward with a poem and this book. A guide, that is meaningful to *you*, with vivid images that *you* connect with. Some of my students took on the challenge of creating some mnemonics and I have included them in this work and credited them in the acknowledgements.

I hope this field guide is something you keep through your board exams and into your practice as a tangible record of this time of exponential learning in your life.

CHAPTER 1 – GASTROINTESTINAL

Peptic ulcer disease

Peptic ulcer disease (PUD) translates loosely to an ulceration of the **peptic** (PEP-tick) or digestive tract. Acid is an aggressive factor in the stomach that, if reduced, may allow an ulcer to heal. An antibiotic may also be used to treat the *Helicobactor pylori*, a helicopter-like organism often found in the ulcer, but in this section we will only focus on three drug classes: The antacid, the H2-blocker and the proton pump inhibitor (PPI).

An antacid is anti-acid without the "i" and is usually composed of a chemical like calcium, magnesium or aluminum.

An H_2 blocker (more formally, H_2 receptor antagonist) stands for histamine two (H_2) blocker. When someone says, "I need an antihistamine", she thinks of allergic symptoms like sneezing, runny nose, etc. Those allergy antihistamines have to do with histamine one (H_1) receptors and we'll cover those in the antihistamine section. Histamine two causes the formation of acid, so blocking it blocks the production of acid.

A proton pump inhibitor (PPI) blocks a pump that introduces protons into the stomach, making it less acidic.

Antacids

Brand names

TUMS – Helps calm your **tum**my, so you can eat food that's yummy.
"TUMS"

MAALOX LIQUID – Take **Ma**gnesium and **Al**uminum hydr**ox**ide, and you'll be able to go on the rides.
"MAY-locks"

MILK OF MAGNESIA – **Magnesi**um + **a**.
"MILK of mag-KNEE-shuh"

ROLAIDS – A **roll** of tablets to **aid** your **s**tomach's frets.
"ROLL-Aids"

Generic names

CALCIUM CARBONATE (Tums)
"CAL-see-um CAR-bow-Nate"

ALUMINUM AND MAGNESIUM HYDROXIDE (Maalox)
"uh-LOU-men-um high-DROCK-side"
"mag-KNEES-e-um high-DROCK-side"

MAGNESIUM HYDROXIDE (Milk of Magnesia)
"mag-KNEES-e-um high-DROCK-side"

CALCIUM CARBONATE AND MAGNESIUM HYDROXIDE (Rolaids)
"CAL-see-um CAR-bow-Nate"
"mag-KNEES-e-um high-DROCK-side"

111111

H$_2$ blockers

Brand names

AXID axes ac**id,** and makes your stomach placid.
"ACK-Sid"

PEPCID reduces **pep**tic **acid**ity, reducing ulcer morbidity.
"PEP-Sid"

TAGAMET an H$_2$ an**tag**onist, an upset stomach, it will assist.
"TAG-uh-met"

ZANTAC - Take **"z" antac**id every 12 hours and you're set.
"ZAN-tack"

Generic names

NIZA<u>TIDINE</u> (Axid)
"Nigh-ZAT-eh-dean"

FAMO<u>TIDINE</u> (Pepcid)
"Fa – MOE – ti – dean"

CIME<u>TIDINE</u> (Tagamet) *some side effes*
"sigh-MET-uh-dean"   *"me too*
                                                          drugs

RANI<u>TIDINE</u> (Zantac)
"Rah-NIT-uh-dean"

H$_2$ blockers use the suffix –tidine.

Proton pump inhibitors

Brand Names

ACIPHEX affects acid, raises **pH,** so you can run the race.
"ASS-effects"

PREVACID prevents **acid** in an hour, so your stomach isn't sour.
"PREV-uh-Sid" *only 1 side*

PRILOSEC creates a **low sec**retion of **pr**otons.
"PRY-low-sec"

PROTONIX nixes protons.
"PRO-tawn-icks"

Generic Names

REBEPRAZOLE (Aciphex)
"Rah-BEP-rah-zole"

LANSOPRAZOLE (Prevacid)
"lan-SEW-pruh-zole"

OMEPRAZOLE (Prilosec)
"oh-MEP-rah-zole"

PANTOPRAZOLE (Protonix)
"pan-TOE-pruh-zole"

Proton Pump Inhibitors use the suffix –prazole.

Poem: Venus Loses her Bite

like the mars rover
attacking the surface
with a fluttering parachute

a purple capsule
splashes the acidic sea
beneath Venusian clouds

untouched landscape
inflamed wrinkle ridges
churning sulfuric eruptions

under the greenhouse
the environmental bomb
smoothes the ocean

quiets volcanic pumps
clears the cloud cover
drops Venus' dress

the goddess spins
naked to stellar winds
carrying microbes

ready to colonize

Venus Loses her Bite. I thought of omeprazole, a drug my daughters had to take and imagined what it would be like in their stomachs. I thought of the hostile environment of the planet Venus. When a proton pump inhibitor is used, the acidic environment that is a barrier to microbes fails.

Constipation, diarrhea, and nausea

Your body's gastrointestinal system often attempts to help protect you by either diluting something toxic or by expelling it, but sometimes we need to override what the body is trying to do. **Diarrhea** can rapidly lead to dehydration and though it is good that the body tries to expel something, sometimes the body goes too far and we need a drug to slow or stop the diarrhea. Also, there are many times where **vomiting** is good, such as when a toxin is present. However, with something like cancer chemotherapy we know what is causing the nausea; we just want to stop it or prevent it.

Constipation is a different matter. Usually constipation comes from some condition that either slows our bowel or is an adverse effect of a drug such as certain *calcium channel blockers* (they block the calcium from getting to the bowel's smooth muscle) or opioids, which are notorious for causing constipation. Often a stool softener is all a patient needs, so be wary of the "I need the fastest thing you've got" because those drugs, like enemas, are really fast and can rapidly lead to dehydration if not used properly or used too often.

Anti-nausea (anti-emetics)

Brand names

EMETROL is for **eme**sis con**trol** and you'll vomit no more.
"EM-eh-trawl"

ZOFRAN uses the o, r, and n from **o**ndanset**ron,** so your
severe nausea will be gone.
"ZO-fran"

Generic names

PHOSPHORATED CARBOHYDRATE (Emetrol)
"FOS-four-ate-id car-bow-HIGH-dreyt"

ONDANSETRON (Zofran)
"on-DAN-se-tron"

Stool softener

Brand name

COLACE improves the **col**on's **pace**, pulls water into the
stool, but doesn't race.
"CO-lace"

Generic name

DOCUSATE SODIUM (Colace)
 "DOCK-you-sate SEWED-e-um"

Anti-diarrheals

Brand names

IMODIUM immobilizes the bowel's **mod**e of transport.
"eh-MOE-Dee-um"

LOMOTIL sl**ow**s the bowel's **motil**ity and alleviates diarrhea.
"LOW-moat-ill"

PEPTO-BISMOL helps with **pept**ic stuff using **bis**muth.
"pep-TOE BIZ-mol"

Generic names

LOPERAMIDE (Imodium)
"Low-PER-uh-mide"

DIPHENOXYLATE/ATROPINE (Lomotil)
"dye-fen-OX-ill-ate / AT-row-peen"

BISMUTH SUBSALICYLATE (Pepto-Bismol)
"BIZ-muth sub-Sal-IS-uh-late"

Ulcerative colitis

Brand name
ASACOL assuages **a col**on with 5-**ASA,** easing a colon's pain today.
"AS-uh-call"

Generic name
MESALAMINE (Asacol)
"meh-SAL-uh-mean"

Gastrointestinal drug practice

Classify these drugs by placing the corresponding drug class letter next to each medication:

1. Calcium carbonate
2. Cimetidine
3. Docusate sodium
4. Famotidine
5. Lansoprazole
6. Loperamide
7. Magnesium hydroxide
8. Mesalamine
9. Omeprazole
10. Ondansetron

Gastrointestinal drug classes:

A. Antacid
B. H_2 blocker
C. Proton pump inhibitor
D. Anti-nausea
E. Stool softener
F. Anti-diarrheal
G. Ulcerative colitis

CHAPTER 2 - MUSCULOSKELETAL

NSAIDs and pain

Non-steroidal anti-inflammatory drugs (NSAIDs) are named that way because many times steroids are used to treat inflammatory conditions. A few NSAIDS such as **aspirin**, **ibuprofen**, and **naproxen** are available over-the-counter and are meant for intermittent pain or conditions that do not require a medical doctor's attention. A drug that relieves pain is called an **analgesic**. A drug that reduces fever is called an **antipyretic**.

The question that comes to the pharmacy is when to use **acetaminophen** (Tylenol) and when to use an **NSAID**. If the patient has inflammation, the acetaminophen will not do anything for them. However, if the patient has pain or fever, then either would be appropriate.

The prescription NSAIDs can be used for specific reasons as prescribed by a doctor such as closing a heart valve (*patent ductus arteriosus*) in a preemie, longer term relief of pain and inflammation, and so forth. The doctor will monitor for specific adverse affects.

Analgesics – NSAIDs

Brand names

ALEVE alleviates pain from strains and sprains.
"uh-LEAVE"

ECOTRIN is enteric coated aspirin.
"ECK-oh-trin"

MOTRIN works a bit like aspirin, cools a headache, drops a fever's vim.
"MO-trin"

INDOCIN is short for **indo**methac**in**, keeps inflammation and pain from a win.
"IN-doe-sin"

Generic names

NAPROXEN (Aleve)
"nap-ROCKS-in"

ASPIRIN (Ecotrin) (ASA)
"AS-per-in"

IBUPROFEN (Motrin)
"eye-byou-PRO-fin"

INDOMETHACIN (Indocin)
"in-doe-METH-uh-sin"

Poem: facts about aspirin

(aspirin with a capital a is trademarked in some places, still)

aspirin does
grow on trees,
willows to be precise,
in the bark.
Hippocrates
knew this
but a person
can't just go
into their backyard,
peel some bark
every time
they have a headache.

Someone had
to make it
into a pill
and someone did
in 1897,
with meadowsweet
to ease the GI upset.

It became
the killer app,
the pipeline darling,
until it lost its patent
in 1917
and anyone
and their chemist mother
could make it.

Like all rock stars,
acetylsalicylic acid,
ASA,
aspirin,
lost to a new generation,
paracetamal,
acetaminophen
in 1956,
then sold
fewer records
after ibuprofen
hit the shelves
in 1969.

When I was a kid,
my parents gave me
delicious
orange flavored
children's aspirin
for my fever.

I know they
didn't mean
to hurt me,
give me
Reye's syndrome,
But, there it was,
a death blow
to aspirin.

The old songs,
they always rise up,
with a new generation
who appreciates them.
Instead of children

leading the charge
 it was the adults,
with bad hearts
clogged arteries,
for aspirin, aside from
reducing fever, pain
and inflammation,
can keeps platelets,
those clotting fragments
from killing
a cardiac patient
and new research
shows it can
prevent certain cancers.

Now, aspirin's
back on the top,
with a new label,
singing again.

facts about aspirin. Dorianne Laux wrote a book of poetry
called "Facts about the Moon." I just took the "facts about"
and added aspirin and took my knowledge of the history of the
evolution of aspirin.

Analgesics – NSAIDs (cont'd)

Brand names

CELEBREX users **celebrate** relief from inflammatory grief.
"SELL-eh-breks"

TORADOL tames **tor**nados of pain, in Latin **dol**or means the same.
"TOUR-uh-doll"

Generic names

KETOROLAC (Toradol)
"key-TOUR-oh-lack"

CELECOXIB (Celebrex)
"sell-eh-COCKS-ib"

Analgesic – non-narcotic

Brand name

TYLENOL comes from the chemical name N-ac**tyl**-para-amino-ph**enol**, that's a mouthful to say it all.
"TIE-Len-all"

Generic name

ACETAMINOPHEN [APAP] (Tylenol)
"uh-seat-uh-MINnow-fin"

Poem: Pharmacoenvironmentology

(The impact of pharmaceuticals and personal care products on the environment)

A vulture picks
at her prey.

Her cooked beak
smiling

Little pecks
bring each atom
belonging
to the bovine
which as good
belongs to her.

She shivers,
loses her breath,
ruffles her feathers,
circles her head
feels her organs
turn to whitish stone.

Pharmacoenvironmentology. Some NSAIDs have been implicated in the deaths of vultures who feed on cows that used the medication. Malaria has a similar effect on vultures and may be the culprit as well. In general, the effects of drugs on the environment are not well studied.

Opioids and narcotics

Opioids are very effective pain relievers (**analgesics**), but they do have the potential for addiction. In the past, some small amounts of **codeine** products were available from the pharmacist directly for patients with a serious cough, but this practice has, for the most part, been discontinued.

The physician will determine which analgesic is best for the particular condition and for how long. Often you will hear about drug schedules and these medications. The **drug schedule** is the DEA's (Drug Enforcement Agency) way of categorizing the addictive potential of the drugs.

Drugs that are *schedule I* are illegal and of no medical value such as **heroin**. *Schedule II* **drugs** are potentially addicting such as **Duragesic** and **Percocet**. *Schedule III* drugs are less addicting and include **Vicodin**. *Schedule IV* drugs include some sleeping pills such as **Ambien** and *schedule V* are often cough medicines that include **codeine**.

Opioid analgesics

Brand names

CODEINE is an alkaloid in opium used to control cough, diminish pain, and deal with diarrhea.
"CO-dean"

DURAGESIC is an anal**gesic**, sometimes in a patch for a long duration.
"dur-uh-GEE-zic"

ENDOCET is **Endo** pharmaceuticals' version of **Percocet**, from a**CET**aminophen comes the cet.
"EN-doe-set"

MORPHINE is named after the god of dreams, **Morpheus** to the Greeks.
"MORE-feen

Generic names

CODEINE
"CO-dean"

FENTANYL (Duragesic)
"FEN-ta-nil"

OXYCODONE/ACETAMINOPHEN (Endocet)
"ox-e-CO-done/ uh-seat-uh-MINnow-fin"

MORPHINE
"MORE-feen"   God of dreams - morpheus

Opioid analgesics

Brand names

*ULTRAM is **ultra**-pain-relieving **tram**adol, how the generic's called.
"ULL-tram"

VICODIN combines hydro**cod**one, a codeine derivative, and acetaminoph**en** you know.
"VIE-co-din"

VICOPROFEN is **vico**din with ibu**profen** instead of acetaminophen.
"vie-co-PRO-fen"

Generic names

*TRAMADOL (Ultram) *– weak opioid*
"TRAM-uh-doll"   *– shouldn't be addictive*

[APAP]
HYDROCODONE/ACETAMINOPHIN (Vicodin) *#1 drug used in country*
"high-droe-CO-done/uh-seat-uh-MINnow-fin"

HYDROCODONE/IBUPROFEN (Vicoprofen)
"high-droe-CO-done/eye-byou-PRO-fin"

*Tramadol (Ultram) weakly affects opioid receptors.

Poem: Five Schedule Cinquain Chain

Schedule
One, addictive
without medical use
heroin, l-s-d, C-1
schedule

schedule
two, addicting
also, medical use
oxycodone, morphine, C-2
schedule

schedule
three, not quite as
bad, still addictive though,
vicodin tabs, C-3
schedule

schedule
four, sleeping pills,
mostly, something like a
zolpidem tab, C-4,
schedule

schedule
five, cough meds taste,
too good sometimes, careful,
APAP – liver, C-5
Schedule

Five Schedule Cinquain Chain. A cinquan poem of the DEA
schedules from I to V.

Headaches and migraines

Common drugs for headache and migraine include the **NSAIDs, Tylenol, caffeine, ergot alkaloids**, and the **triptans.**

NSAIDS make sense because they reduce inflammation and one cause of headache is thought to be a swelling of the vessels in the brain. **Tylenol** is a pain reliever and also makes sense. **Caffeine** seems like a strange drug to have in a headache preparation, but caffeine is a potent vasoconstrictor (makes blood vessels narrower) and it is thought to narrow swollen vessels in the brain. **Ergot alkaloids** function in part by using vasoconstriction and also binding to a specific receptor in the brain. **Triptan**, the suffix of the drugs in a **5-HT receptor agonist** class, work by activating receptors that reduce certain swelling associated with migraines. They are called *triptans* because two syllables, the last in the generic names of these drugs, are simply easier to say than **5-hydroxytryptamine receptor agonists.**

Drugs for headache and migraine

Brand names

AXERT can help **AX** and ex**ERT** its' effects against a
migraine that hurts.
"AKS-ert"

EXCEDRIN exceptionally combines caffeine, acetaminophen,
and aspi**rin,** to keep your head from throbbing.
"ECKS-said-rin"

IMITREX wrecks imminent migraine pain.
"IM-eh-treks"

MIGRANAL is for **migraine** headache y'all.
"MY-gran-all"

Generic names

ALMOTRIPTAN (Axert) – migraine drug
"Al-Mo-TRIP-tan"
↗ inflammation   ↗ additional   ↗ potentent vasal constriction
   AsA   / APAP   analgesic
ASPIRIN/ACETAMINOPHEN/CAFFEINE (Excedrin)
"AS-per-in/uh-seat-uh-MINnow-fin/ka-FEEN"   ↳ or for headache

SUMATRIPTAN (Imitrex)
"Sue-ma-TRIP-tan"

DIHYDROERGOTAMINE (Migranal)
"dye-high-droe-er-GOT-uh-mean"

*The suffix –triptan signifies a 5-HT receptor agonist, a
migraine medication.*

Poem: Aspirin

Aspirin does grow on trees,
in the bit of willow bark
I reach for each morning
to cool my headaches.

The willow's roots
under my front yard
reach into my basement,
curl into a pipe,

And drink
until the water's gone.

Aspirin. My grandparents had a huge willow tree in their front
yard that got into his pipes and I thought of the way a headache
crawls into a person's head.

DMARDs and rheumatoid arthritis

DMARDs stands for **d**isease-**m**odifying **a**nti**r**heumatic **drugs**, which means they work against **rheumatoid arthritis**, an autoimmune disorder where the person's own immune system causes pain and inflammation. These drugs reduce the progression of the disease as opposed to the treatment of **osteoarthritis**, a condition where the body has worn down and the joints are inflamed. Both conditions respond to a reduction in inflammation through the use of NSAIDs (non-steroidal anti-inflammatory drugs) such as ibuprofen (**Motrin**) or aspirin (**ASA**). Glucocorticoids, such as prednisone, can further help reduce inflammation. Special immune-suppressing drugs like etanercept (**Enbrel**), methotrexate (**Rheumatrex**), or inflixamab (**Remicaide**) are used for autoimmune diseases.

Be careful not to confuse *osteoarthritis*, a joint disease, with *osteoporosis*, which is a thinning or reduction in the density of the bone tissue. Drugs for **osteoporosis** help build the bone back up. Because bone growth is so slow, certain drugs can be given once a month such as ibandronate (**Boniva**).

DMARDs and an anti-inflammatory steroid

Brand names

* **DELTA<u>SONE</u>** is like predni**sone**, stops inflammation and eases rheumatic bones.
"DEALT-uh-sewn"

ENBREL enables arthritics to find **rel**ief.
"EN-brell"

REMICADE remediates and **aid**s against autoimmune raids.
"REM-eh-kaid"

RHEUMATREX is an anti**rheumat**ic whose generic name is metho**trex**ate.
"ROOM-uh-treks"

Generic names

* **PREDNI<u>SONE</u>** (Deltasone) – *anti-inflammatory steroid*
"PRED-ni-sewn"

ETANERCEPT (Enbrel) – *DMARD*
"eh-TAN-er-sept"   – *severe arthritis*

INFLIXI<u>MAB</u> (Remicade)
"in-FLICKS-eh-mab"

METHOTREXATE (Rheumatrex) *Meth o T-Rex ate* the rheumatic inflammate.
"meth-oh-TREKS-ate"

*The suffix –sone often indicates a steroid type drug.
*The suffix – mab stands for **monoclonal antibody**.*

Gout

Brand names

CHOLCRYS clears gouty **crystals** in big toes and other places.
"COAL-Chris"

ULORIC lowers uric acid levels, helping fight the gout devil.
"YOU-lore-ick"

ZYLOPRIM lowers uric acid to **prevent** a long gouty torrent.
"ZY-low-prim"

Generic names

COLCHICINE (Cholcrys)
"COAL-che-seen"

FEBUXOSTAT (Uloric)
"fe-BUCKS-oh-stat"

ALLOPURINOL (Zyloprim) → prevents uric acid
"aloe-PURE-in-all"

Osteoporosis agents

Brand names

BONIVA returns **bone's** life or **vida** if Spanish is your spice.
"bo-KNEE-vuh"

FOSAMAX replaces the **bone fossa** to the **max,** careful wait 30 minutes before you lay down to relax.
"FA-seh-max"

MIACALCIN puts **my calcium** back in my bones, so they won't crack.
"MY-uh-Cal-sin"

OS-CAL adds the bone prefix **O-S**, with **-cal**, for **cal**cium.
"OZ-cal"

Generic names 7 suffix -helps w/ osteoporosis

IBANDRONATE (Boniva)
"eh-BAND-row-Nate"

ALENDRONATE (Fosamax)
"uh-LEN-dro-Nate"

CALCITONIN (Miacalcin)
"Cal-si-TONE-in"

 CALCIUM CARBONATE (Os-Cal)
"CAL-see-um CAR-bow-Nate"

The suffix -dronate is a bisphosphonate used for osteoporosis.

Musculoskeletal drug practice

Classify these drugs by placing the corresponding drug class letter next to each medication:

1. Acetaminophen
2. Alendronate
3. ASA/APAP/caffeine
4. Colchicine
5. Etanercept
6. Fentanyl
7. Hydrocodone/APAP
8. Ibuprofen
9. Prednisone
10. Sumatriptan

Musculoskeletal Drug Classes:

A. NSAID
B. Non-narcotic analgesic
C. Opioid analgesic
D. Opioid analgesic
E. 5HT receptor agonist for headache
F. Non-narcotic analgesic combo - headache
G. Steroid/anti-inflammatory
H. DMARD/TNF inhibitor
I. Bisphosphonate for osteoporosis
J. Anti-gout

CHAPTER 3 – RESPIRATORY

Antihistamines, asthma, and cough

Antihistamines are divided into two generations: First and second. The first and older generation would make patients sleepy. Drugs such as diphenydramine (**Benadryl**) are still used as antihistamines and also as an over-the-counter sleep aid. The new generation cannot pass through the blood-brain-barrier and cause no or minimal drowsiness. Drugs in this class include fexofenadine (**Allegra**) and loratadine (**Claritin**).

Asthma, in short, can be thought of as a disease of inflammation and bronchoconstriction; that is, the branches of the lung start to tighten. Drugs for asthma will affect one or both of these conditions. For example, albuterol (**ProAir**) will help with the bronchoconstriction. However, the combination product fluticasone/salmeterol (**Advair**) will provide relief from both.

Cough can be prevented with an over-the-counter medication dextromethorphan (**Robitussin DM**) and severe cases might require a codeine-based product such as **Robitussin with Codeine.**

Antihistamine

Brand names

ALLEGRA mixes up the letters in "**allergy**," makes a word that means happy.
"uh-LEG-rah"

*BENADRYL benefits you by **dry**ing up your runny nose.
"BEN-uh-drill"

CLARITIN clears allergy symptoms, so you can go outside and breathe the air **in**.
 "KLAR-eh-tin"

ZYRTEC provides **tech**nical allergy relief all year.
"ZEER-tech"

Generic names

FEXOFENADINE (Allegra)
"fex-oh-FEN-uh-dean"

*DIPHENHYDRAMINE (Benadryl)
"dye-fen-HIGH-dra-mean"

LORATADINE (Claritin)
"lore-AT-uh-dean"

CETIRIZINE (Zyrtec)
"seh-TIRE-uh-zine"

*Diphenhydramine (Benadryl) is a first-generation antihistamine which is usually more sedating than the second-generation drugs Allegra, Claritin, and Zyrtec.

Poem: Antihistamine

A volcano sputters,
quiets

a running lava flow
crisps

ash winds dust
caverns

an angry peak
resists

Antihistamine. I thought of what happens to a patient's nose
when that person takes an antihistamine: The sneezing and
runny nose stops. There is also a drying effect and the nose, a
bit weathered from the storm, takes time to settle.

Asthma

Brand names

ADVAIR adds two drugs to reduce an asthmatic's **air**flow plugs.
"ADD-vair"

ATROVENT ventilates with ip**ratro**pium, so you can breathe again.
"AT-row-vent"

AZMACORT is a **cort**icosteroid for **asthma**.
"AZ-muh-court"

BRETHAIRE helps an asthmatic **breathe air**.
"BREATH-air"

Generic names

FLUTICA<u>SONE</u>/SALME<u>TEROL</u> (Advair)
"flue-TIC-uh-sewn/Sal-MEET-er-all"

IPRATROPIUM (Atrovent)
"i-pra-TROW-pee-um"

TRIAMCINO<u>LONE</u> (Azmacort)
"try-am-SIN-oh-lone"

TERBUTALINE (Brethaire)
"ter-BYOU-ta-lean"

The suffix –terol indicates a bronchodilator.
The suffix – sone/-lone indicates a steroid.

Asthma (cont'd)

Brand names

PROAIR **pro**vides **air** to asthmatics, so they can do gymnastics.
"PRO-air"

SINGULAIR is taken one **single** time a day, to improve **air**flow so kids can go out and play.
"SING-you-lair"

Generic names

ALBU<u>TEROL</u> (ProAir)
"Al-BYOU-ter-all"

MONTELUKAST (Singulair)
"Monte-LUKE-ast"

The suffix –terol indicates a bronchodilator.

Cough

ROBITUSSIN DM is an anti**tuss**ive.
"row-bi-TUSS-in"

Generic names

GUAIFENESIN/DEXTROMETHORPHAN (Robitussin DM)
"gwhy-FEN-uh-sin/decks-trow-meh-THOR-fan"

Guaifenesin is a mucolytic, breaking up mucous and dextromethorphan, the DM, represents the cough suppressant.

Classify these drugs by placing the corresponding drug class letter next to each medication:

1. Albuterol
2. Cetirizine
3. Diphenhydramine
4. Fluticasone/salmeterol
5. Guaifenesin/DM
6. Ipratropium
7. Loratadine
8. Montelukast
9. Terbutaline
10. Triamcinolone

Respiratory drug classes:

A. First-generation antihistamine
B. Second-generation antihistamine
C. Mucolytic/cough suppressant
D. Steroid/anti-inflammatory/long-acting bronchodilator
E. Anticholinergic for asthma
F. Steroid/anti-inflammatory
G. Beta$_2$ agonist
H. Short-acting bronchodilator
I. Leukotriene receptor antagonist

CHAPTER 4 – IMMUNE SYSTEM

Antimicrobials in a nutshell

Antimicrobials can be further divided into **antibiotics** (drugs against bacteria), **antifungals** (drugs against mycoses or fungi), or **antivirals**, drugs that work against viruses and there are other organisms as well. I'm not going to review all the different ways these drugs can work, I just want to show how, in this particular class of drugs, prefixes and suffixes are especially prevalent to help you remember which is which.

Suffixes:

> **-azole** – Antifungal [do not confuse with -prazole]
> **-cillin** – Penicillin antibiotic
> **-cycline** – Tetracycline antibiotic
> **-floxacin** – Fluoroquinolone antibiotic
> **-micin, mycin** – Possible aminoglycoside antibiotic
> [not -*thromycin*]
> **-thromycin** – Macrolide antibiotic
> **-vir** – Antiviral

Prefixes:

> **Sulfa** – Sulfa antibiotic.
> **Cef-, Ceph** – Cephalosporin antibiotic

Antibiotics: Penicillins

Brand names

AMOXIL is from **amoxi**cillin, bacteria it does the killin'.
"uh-MOCKS-ill"

AUGMENTIN augments amoxicill**in**'s defense against a
beta-lactamase offense.
"og-MENT-in"

Generic names

AMOXICILLIN (Amoxil)
"uh-mocks-eh-SILL-in"

AMOXICILLIN/CLAVULANATE (Augmentin)
"uh-mocks-eh-SILL-in/clav-you-LAWN-ate"

Penicillins have the suffix –cillin.

Antibiotics: Cephalosporins

Brand names

FORTAZ is not **four**th but third-generation, the cephalosporin ce**ftaz**idime for bacterial infection.
"FOUR-taz"

KEFLEX is the first-generation cephalosporin c**eph**a**lex**in.
"KE-flecks"

MAXIPIME is a fourth-generation cephalosporin, the **max** generation, of generic cefe**pime**.
"MAX-eh-peem"

ROCEPHIN is Hoffman-La**Ro**che's patent, a third-generation **ceph**alospor**in** antibacterial combatant.
"row-SEF-in"

Generic names

CEFTAZIDIME (Fortaz)
"sef-TAZ-eh-deem"

CEPHALEXIN (Keflex)
"sef-uh-LEX-in"

CEFEPIME (Maxipime)
"SEF-eh-peem"

CEFTRIAXONE (Rocephin)
"sef-try-AX-own"

Cephalosporins use cef- or ceph- for a prefix.

Antibiotics: Macrolides

Brand names

BIAXIN is like erythromycin, but given **b.i.d.**, or half as often.
"bi-AX-in"

E-MYCIN is short for the generic erythro**mycin,** that puts up a fight against bacterial invasion.
"E-MY-sin"

ZITHROMAX uses the generic a**zith**romycin's letters, to provide **max**imum antibiotic coverage.
"ZITH-row-max"

Generic names

✓ **CLARITHROMYCIN** (Biaxin)
  "Claire-ITH-row-my-sin"

✗ **ERYTHROMYCIN** (E-Mycin)
  "err-ITH-row-my-sin"

✗ **AZITHROMYCIN** (Zithromax)
  "a-ZITH-row-my-sin"

Macrolides have the suffix –thromycin.

Antibiotics: Fluoroquinolones

Brand names

AVELOX has the **-lox** root of a -floxacin, the suffix that means a fluoroquinolone you're takin'.
"AVE-uh-locks"

CIPRO brand name cuts the –floxacin from **cipro**floxacin.
"SIP-row"

LEVAQUIN is the brand name for the fluoro**quin**olone antibiotic **levo**floxacin.
"LEV-uh-Quinn"

Generic names

X **CIPROFLOXACIN** (Cipro)
"sip-row-FLOCKS-uh-sin"

X **LEVOFLOXACIN** (Levaquin)
"Lee-vo-FLOCKS-uh-sin"

MOXIFLOXACIN (Avelox)
"Mocks-e-FLOCKS-uh-sin"

Fluoroquinolone antibiotics use the suffix -floxacin

Antibiotics: Aminoglycosides

Brand names

AMIKIN takes a prefix and suffix from **amikacin,** an aminoglycoside bacteria don't want to find themselves facin'. "AM-eh-kin"

GARAMYCIN is short for **gentamicin**, but spelled with **my** instead of **-micin**. "gare-uh-MY-sin"

Generic names

X **AMIKACIN** (Amikin) "am-eh-KAY-sin"

X **GENTAMICIN** (Garamycin) "Jenn-ta-MY-sin"

Aminoglycosides can use the suffix –mycin or –micin, be wary of macrolides that end in –thromycin, vancomycin and clindamycin which are not aminoglycosides.

Poem: A Pair of Antimicrobial Haikus

Gentamicin, an
aminoglycoside for
eyes pink – not happy.

Acyclovir tames
herpes on lip, on skin or
down, down, down, down there

A Pair of Antimicrobial Haikus. I wrote about thirty Haikus,
but these two were my favorites. Gentamicin is an
aminoglycoside antibiotic to treat "pink eye" and acyclovir can
be used to treat genital herpes – down, down, down there.

Antibiotics: Tetracyclines

Brand names

DORYX is **doxy**cycline, sure is a tetracycline.
"DOOR-icks"

Generic names

DOXYCYCLINE (Doryx)
"docks-e-SIGH-clean"

Tetracyclines use the suffix –cycline.

Antibiotics: Lincosamide

Brand names

CLEOCIN is short for **cl**indamy**cin**, clears up acne so you can grin.
 "KLEE-oh-sin"

Generic names

CLINDAMYCIN (Cleocin)
"clin-duh-MY-sin"

Antibiotic: Nitroimidazole / Anti-protozoal

Brand name

FLAGYL is the pill that kills *Clostridium **Difficile**.*
"FLADGE-ill"

Generic name

METRONIDAZOLE (Flagyl)
"met-ruh-NID-uh-zole"

Antibiotic: Glycopeptide

Brand name

VANCOCIN is for MRSA, sometimes a last resort, so we
don't always give it away.
"VAN-co-sin"

Generic name

VANCOMYCIN (Vancocin)
"van-co-MY-sin"

Antibiotic: Sulfa / Dihidrofolate reductase inhibitor

Brand name

SMZ/TMP is the acronym for the sulfamethoxazole/trimethoprim, a mouthful to say, but it will clear your urine and save the day.
"s-m-zee/tea-m-pea"

Generic name

SULFAMETHOXAZOLE/TRIMETHOPRIM (SMZ-TMP)
"sull-fa-meth-OX-uh-zole/try-METH-oh-prim"

Sulfa drugs use the prefix sulfa-.

Anti-tuberculosis agents

Brand names

INH is an acronym for **iso**n**i**cotinyl**h**ydrazine, a TB drug's name, few longer we've seen.
"EYE-en-h"

MYAMBUTOL is the **my**cobacterium fighting TB drug eth**ambutol**.
"my-AM-byou-tall"

PZA is the acronym for the TB drug **p**yra**z**in**a**mide.
"pee-zee-a"

RIFADIN is short for the generic TB drug **rif**amp**in**.
"rif-UH-din"

Generic names

ISONIAZID (INH)
"eye-sew-NIGH-uh-zid"

ETHAMBUTOL (Myambutol)
"eh-THAM-byou-tall

PYRAZINAMIDE (PZA)
"pier-uh-ZIN-uh-mide"

RIFAMPIN (Rifadin)
"rif-AMP-in"

Antifungals

Brand names

DIFLUCAN uses the first two syllables of **flucon**azole, to kill fungi, that's it's role.
"die-FLUE-can"

FUNGIZONE kills systemic **fungi**.
"FUN-gah-zone"

LAMISIL can be used to **lam**inate a toenail fungus.
"LAMB-eh-sill"

MYCOSTATIN uses the suffix from **nystatin**, the generic name and prefix **Myco**, meaning fungus.

Generic names

FLUCONAZOLE (Diflucan)
"flue-CON-uh-zole"

AMPHOTERICIN B (Fungizone)
"am-foe-TER-uh-sin Bee"

TERBINAFINE (Lamisil)
"ter-BIN-uh-feen"

NYSTATIN (Mycostatin)
"NIGH-stat-in"

Antifungals have classes or types: Fluconazole is a triazole, amphotericin B and nystatin are polyenes, and terbinafine is an allylamine.

Antivirals

Brand names

ABREVA abbreviates how long a cold sore lasts, so you can get that first kiss, if you are asked.
"uh-BREE-vugh"

FAMVIR short for the **fam**ciclovir, kills a virus without peer.
"FAM-veer"

RELENZA represses influ**enza** virus and that is desirous.
"rah-LEN-zuh"

RETROVIR kills **retrovir**uses like HIV, usually with these drugs, you need three.
"REH-tro-veer"

Generic names

DOCOSANOL (Abreva)
"DO-co-san-all"

FAMCICLOVIR (Famvir)
"fam-SIGH-clo-veer"

ZANAMIVIR (Relenza)
"za-NAH-mi-veer"

ZIDOVUDINE (Retrovir)
"zie-DOE-view-dean"

Drugs used to combat viruses usually have the suffix –vir. Docosanol and famciclovir are generally for herpes virus, zanamivir for influenza, and zidovudine for HIV.

Antivirals (cont'd)

Brand names

TAMIFLU tames in**flu**enza.
"TA-mi-flue"

VALTREX is **val**acyclovir plus **t-rex,** and wrecks a virus.
"VAL-trex"

ZOVIRAX axes **zo**ster **vir**us.
"zo-VIE-racks"

Generic names

OSELTAMI<u>VIR</u> (Tamiflu)
"owe-sell-TAM-eh-veer"

VALACYCLO<u>VIR</u> (Valtrex)
"Val-uh-SIGH-clo-veer"

ACYCLO<u>VIR</u> (Zovirax)
"a-SIGH-clo-veer"

Drugs used to combat viruses usually have the suffix –vir. Generally oseltamivir is for influenza, valacyclovi, and acyclovir are for herpes virus.

Song: Antimicrobial March

(To: When Johnny comes
Marching Home)

Amoxicillin, a penicillin,
Broad-spectrum drug

Clindamycin clears your acne, like
Doxycycline does,

Erythromycin and a Z-Pak
two macrolides keep you on track
Like gentamicin
Fighting gram negative back

Acyclovir for simplex virus,
Five times, a day

Vancomycin, a last resort
M-R-S-A

Ceftriaxone, cephalexin
Generations three and one,
And ciprofloxin
Makes sure UTI is done

With metronidazole be sure
No alcohol,

S-M-Z T-M-P makes fol-
-ic acid stall,

Itraconazole kills fungi now
To cefprozil, bacteria bow,
And hepatitis,
Hates interferon.

Immune drug practice

Classify these drugs by placing the corresponding drug class letter next to each medication:

1. Amoxicillin
2. Azithromycin
3. Cefepime
4. Ceftriaxone
5. Fluconazole
6. Gentamicin
7. Isoniazid
8. Levofloxacin
9. Nystatin
10. Valacyclovir

Immune drug classes:

A. Antibiotic: Penicillin
B. Antibiotic: Fourth-generation cephalosporin
C. Antibiotic: Third-generation cephalosporin
D. Antibiotic: Macrolide
E. Antibiotic: Fluoroquinolone
F. Antibiotic: Aminoglycoside
G. Anti-tuberculosis
H. Anti-fungal: Triazole
I. Anti-fungal- polyene
J. Anti-viral (herpes)

CHAPTER 5 – NERVOUS SYSTEM

Sedative-hypnotics (sleeping pills)

Brand names

AMBIEN creates an **ambient**, sleepy environment.
"AM-bee-en"

BENADRYL puts patients that have been awake in a **dream**-like drowsy state.
"BEN-uh-drill"

LUNESTA uses the Latin for moon (**Luna**) and r**est**.
"Lou-NES-tuh"

RESTORIL is a **rest** helping **pill** that **restores** yourself.
"RES-tour-ill"

Generic names

ZOLPIDEM (Ambien)
"ZOLE-pi-dem"

DIPHENHYDRAMINE (Benadryl)
"dye-fen-HIGH-dra-mean"

ESZOPICLONE (Lunesta)
"es-zo-PEH-clone"

TEMAZEPAM (Restoril)
"te-MAZE-eh-pam"

Sedative/hypnotics (sleeping pills) (cont'd)

Brand names

ROZEREM helps you get **REM** (rapid eye movement) sleep and your **z**'s, with that, you must be pleased.
"row-ZER-em"

SECONAL is short for **seco**barbit**al,** a barbiturate that does not at all, let you stay awake.
"SEC-oh-nal"

Generic names

RAMELTEON (Rozerem)
"ram-ELL-tea-on"

SECOBARBITAL (Seconal)
"see-co-BARB-it-all / sec-oh-BARB-it-all"

Poem: If I could give my kids a Zolpidem

If I could give my kids a zolpidem
No. They're 11 years too young
They can't fall asleep
How about just one?
What about temazepam?
They don't stay asleep.
Maybe I'll take one of those
so I don't hear a peep
I know I can't do either,
suffering I must do
Now my parents laugh it up
Ha. Look at you

If I could give my kids a Zolpidem. There are two general classes of sleep aid, or hypnotic: Those that help a patient fall asleep, like zolpidem, or those that help a patient stay asleep, like temazepam. Obviously, I can't give an infant a sleep aid and I can't take one either because I have to be up, so my parents can get a laugh out of me having to go through child rearing.

Three classes of antidepressant

SSRIs/TCAs/MAOIs

Many students are intimidated by the length of the names of the antidepressant drug classes. All one has to do is break down the word to figure out what it does. The first class is the **selective serotonin reuptake inhibitor (SSRI)** which includes drugs such as **Celexa, Paxil**, and **Prozac**. This drug will inhibit, or block the reuptake (breakdown) of serotonin. If there is more serotonin around, then the mood should be elevated.

The second group of drugs is named not after the transmitter it affects, but what the chemical structure looks like. A **tricyclic antidepressant (TCA)** has three rings and an example is **Elavil**, meant to elevate one's mood.

The last group includes the **monoamine oxidase inhibitors (MAOIs)**. A word that ends in –ase is usually an enzyme so if an antidepressant blocks the enzyme, then that monoamine neurotransmitter must be a neurotransmitter, elevating mood. An example is **Nardil**.

Selective serotonin reuptake inhibitors (SSRIs)

Brand names

CELEXA starts with a "**c**", like the generic citalopram, and can **relax** depression and anxiety.
"SELL-ex-uh"

PAXIL takes **p-a-x-i** from **pa**roxetine.
"PACKS-ill"

PROZAC provides **exactly** what a depressed patient needs.
"PRO-Zack"

ZOLOFT lofts a depressed patient's mood.
"ZO-loft"

Generic names

CITALOPRAM (Celexa)
"sit-AL-oh-pram"

PAROXETINE (Paxil)
"par-OX-eh-teen"

FLUOXETINE (Prozac)
"flue-VOX-uh-mean"

SERTRALINE (Zoloft)
"SIR-tra-lean"

Poem: Inside the Antidepressant Factory

(Eli Lilly and Company, Group Tour, Birthplace of Prozac ®, Indianapolis, Indiana)

The gaggle bumps through a field trip, move along,
through the corridors, stark geometric buildings, young
docs ready to jump ship, explore, make their own
tour, their own serotonin surge somewhere, but no,

keep hands and arms inside, don't touch the glass, yes,
those are real people working, no more bovine and porcine
pancreatic product here, made it human with shiny new
recombinant technology cold packed for freshness,

time to move along, somewhere behind a key coded
door, the heroes of happiness, presenting pulchritude
to the masses, work the pipeline, not on the tour,
not available for autographs, thanks for coming,

a serotinergic snack available at a store near you,
would have liked to have had a bite, to tear through
Midwestern clouds locking arms, forming a phalanx
against the burning luminary trapped 'till May.

Inside the Antidepressant Factory. Prozac was invented by Eli

Lilly and Co. and when my class went on tour there it was

depressingly gray. Lilly also makes human insulin. While on

tour we really wanted to meet the scientists behind the drug.

Prozac was the first in a class of antidepressant drugs known as

the selective serotonin reuptake inhibitors.

Tricyclic antidepressants

ELAVIL can **elevate** your mood.
"Elle-uh-vill"

TOFRANIL can return your happy will.
"TOE-fruh-nil"

AMITRIPTYLINE (Elavil)
"ah-meh-TRIP-ta-lean"

IMIPRAMINE (Tofranil)
"IM-ip-ruh-mean"

Monoamine oxidase inhibitors (MAOIs)

Brand Names

MARPLAN alleviates **ma**jor depression, so you can keep your **plan**s and make a good impression.
"MAR-Plan"

NARDIL's A is in the middle of **M A**nd **O**, **I** say.
"NAR-dill"

PARNATE
"PAR-Nate"

Generic Names

ISOCARBOXAZID (Marplan) is for atypical sad man who laments, "I so carve boxes."
"iso-car-BOX-uh-zid"

PHENELZINE (Nardil)
"FEN-uhl-zine"

TRANYLCYPROMINE (Parnate)
"tran-ill-SIP-row-mean"

Benzodiazepines and ADHD medications

Benzodiazepines are generally used for anxiety or muscle relaxation. They are named not after a neurotransmitter they affect, but like the tricyclic antidepressants, after their chemical structure which is a combination of a benzene ring and a diazepine ring. Because the word **benzodiazepine** has so many syllables, most people just call them **benzos**. Examples include **Valium** and **Xanax**.

While one might think that **ADHD** (attention-deficit-hyperactivity disorder) medications, which are generally stimulants, would be opposite benzodiazepines in their function, they do something similar. They create calm in a person who has a hyperactive mind and/or body without the sedative effect. Examples include **Adderall** and **Concerta**.

Benzodiazepines

Brand names

ATIVAN is a benzo variety that likes **vanquishing** anxiety.
"AT-eh-van"

KLONOPIN uses the phonetic spelling of **clonazepam's** prefix -**clon**.
"KLON-uh-pin"

VALIUM helps relax you like the root **val**erian.
"VAL-e-um"

XANAX "x's" out **anx**iety.
"ZAN-ax"

Generic names

LORA<u>ZEPAM</u> (Ativan)
"lore-A's-eh-Pam"

CLONA<u>ZEPAM</u> (Klonopin)
"klah-NAZ-uh-Pam"

DIA<u>ZEPAM</u> (Valium)
"dye-A's-eh-Pam"

ALPRA<u>ZOLAM</u> (Xanax) has one z, benzodiazepine has two, Xanax sounds like a z, to help you get a snooz.
"Al-PRAY-zo-lamb"

Benzodiazepines often use -zolam and –zepam as suffixes.

ADHD medications

Brand names

ADDERALL helps a student give it **her all**.
"ADD-er-all"

CONCERTA can help a patient **concentrate**.
"con-CERT-uh"

FOCALIN helps a patient **focus**.
"FOE-ca-lin"

*STRATTERA helps **stra**ighten patients' **atte**ntion.
"stra-TER-uh"

Generic names

METHYLPHENIDATE/ DEXMETHYLPHENIDATE
(Adderall)
"meth-ill-FEN-eh-date/dex-meth-ill-FEN-eh-date"

METHYLPHENIDATE (Concerta)
"meth-ill-FEN-eh-date"

DEXMETHYLPHENIDATE (Focalin)
"dex-meth-ill-FEN-eh-date"

*ATOMOXETINE (Strattera)
"a-to-MOCKS-e-teen"

*Atomoxetine (Strattera) is a non-stimulant medication; all others on this page are stimulants. Stimulants can also be used for narcolepsy and, rarely, weight loss.

Poem: Night Pointillism

Touch Seurat's Sunday
Island Afternoon
Feel the dots paint
your fingerprint

Color Chicago's winds
with an open palm
Dirty the El's doors
with Yellow 36

Flee the city
with a red flashlight
Plant where Edison's
lit fingers can't reach.

Meet the gray *seas*
rain, *serenity*
Fall, drown in
the *billowy bay*

Wrap yourself round
Messier's thirty-first –
pixels patient to reach
Chandrasekhar's limit

Poem: ADHD: It's Fake

ADHD.
It's fake.
A doctor's word.
A made up disease.
Bad parents give ADHD drugs.
Bad parents who are too busy.
Bad parents who want a quick fix.
Bad parents who want their kids compliant, sedate.
If parents spent more time, all would be fine.
Home school them for a while, then send them in.
Dexmethylphenidate dad and methylphenidate mom, great foster parents for latchkey kids.
No, I don't have a child diagnosed with ADHD, but I know.

Poem: ADHD: It's Real

ADHD.
It's real.
Ask the DSM-IV.
A bona fide syndrome.
Good parents give ADHD drugs.
Good parents who do care enough.
Good parents who checked all the options.
 Good parents don't want to feed kids amphetamines.
It's like the pesticides and honeybees – dizzy and dying.
Colony collapse disorder for kids, don't know what causes it.
Congress won't help the honeybees; I can't imagine they'll help us.
Yes. I have a child diagnosed with ADHD, and I don't know.

Night Pointillism. Someone mentioned Adderall XR and the spheres inside. I thought of Seurat's pointillism painting housed in Chicago, then to a field at night (astronomers use red lights to keep from ruining their night vision) away from the city lights (Edison), watching the man in the moon, the eyes are translated to rain and serenity, the nose to billowy bay, then a spiral galaxy made up of the little points of stars, some of which might burst from Chandrasekhar's limit as to how large a dwarf star can get. Often ADHD patients drift in their thinking and I wanted to comment on how those thoughts tend to be vivid adventures.

ADHD: It's Fake. ADHD: It's Real. This was an assignment that asked us to write something that we were angry about using one word, then two words, until we got to twelve words. A prior psychology professor cleverly allowed students to argue if ADHD is fake or real and that's what these mirror poems are about. The outcry from parents of ADHD children made online class history. ADHD, to me, is a strange thing because it didn't exist when I was younger so I feel like something had to happen between then, the early 80s, and now. There is something called colony collapse disorder that started killing honeybees and it was eventually attributed to a pesticide. I expect that when researches do figure out what causes ADHD, they will find there is something toxic.

Schizophrenia

Brand names

ABILIFY gives schizophrenic patients the **ability**
to manage their state and that's first rate.
"uh-BILL-eh-FIE"

*HALDOL is **hal**operi**dol**, an anti-psychotic first of all.
"HAL-doll"

LITHIUM is in the same group as Natr**ium** (Na) – sodium –
and where the salt goeth, the lithium goeth too.
"LITH-e-um"

RISPERDAL is **risper**idone, an antipsychotic, that is known.
"RIS-per-doll"

Generic names

ARIPIPRAZOLE (Abilify)
"eh-reh-PIP-rah-zole"

*HALOPERIDOL (Haldol)
"hallow-PEAR-eh-doll"

LITHIUM
"LITH-e-um"

RISPERIDONE (Risperdal)
"ris-PEAR-eh-doen"

**Haloperidol is a first-generation (typical) antipsychotic.
Lithium is a salt; the other two are second-generation
(atypical) antipsychotics.*

Poem: Denied the Living Room

If I take the pill by my bed, I will
Fall asleep.
If I fall asleep, I will want
To dream.
If I begin to dream, I will not want
To wake.
If I do not wake, I will not make it to the
Living room.
What choice, do
I have?

If I take the other pill, I will not
Sit still.
If I cannot sit still, I will not want
To sleep.
If I do not sleep, I will want to go to the
Living room.
But I am embarrassed to go to the living room,
With my tics.
So I will have to lie in bed, where I cannot
Sit still.

Denied the Living Room. This poem was inspired by Alberto
Rios' poem "Dangerous Shirt". Often a person taking a first-
generation antipsychotic has to decide if they want to take a
drug that is sedating or causes extrapyramidal symptoms (tics),
if they get to decide at all, or an atypical antipsychotic which
usually has long term metabolic effects.

Poem: Renga with my Id

I do not want to
Take the poison – it will kill
My muse and my gift,
I will be ordinary
Again, just three dash two dash four.

Can't leave me without
It – I'm your shadow ever
and always without
your poison – take it and I
die, but you die also – choose.

I can't decide,
Diagnosed dysfunctional
Am I, another
Will choose, I'm at the mercy
Of their logic and the doctor's.

Make a rational
choice? About invisible
men? Voices they can't
hear? they will always choose life,
handing death to us both.

Renga with my Id. A renga is a type of poem usually written
between two people. In this poem I changed it around to a
person who is talking with their schizophrenic self. Some very
famous creative people have had schizophrenia and when they
are treated, their gift is lost. The doctor and family choose
death to the creativity, that the person will live a "normal" life.

Antiepileptics

Brand names

DEPAKOTE controls convulsions and uses five from
Dival**p**r**o**ex.
"DEP-uh-coat"

DILANTIN uses three letters of phe**n**yto**in**, to stop a patient
from shaking.
"DYE-lan-tin"

GABITRIL uses five letters from **t**i**agab**ine, to con**t**r**ol**
seizures is what I mean.
"GAB-uh-trill"

KEPPRA **pr**events **ep**ileptic attacks.
"KEPP-rah"

Generic names

DIVALPROEX (Depakote)
"dye-Val-PRO-ex"

PHENYTOIN (Dilantin)
"FEN-eh-toyn"

TIAGABINE (Gabitril)
"tie-AH-ga-bean"

LEVETIRACETAM (Keppra)
"le-ve-teer-UH-seat-am"

*Divalproex and Phenytoin are considered traditional anti-
epileptic drugs. Tiagabine and levetiracetam are newer drugs.*

Antiepileptics (cont'd)

Brand names

LAMICTAL lessens ton**ic**-clon**ic** seizures it seems, and uses the first three letters of **lam**otrigine.
"LAMB-ick-tall"

LYRICA can put neurons back in **lyric** rhythm and control.
"LEER-eh-ca"

NEURONTIN affects **neur**onal pulsing, uses the last four letters of gabape**ntin.**
"NER-on-tin"

TEGRETOL con**trol**s seizures.
"TEG-reh-tawl"

Generic names

LAMOTRIGINE (Lamictal)
"la-MO-tri-Gene"

PREGABALIN (Lyrica)
"pre-GAB-uh-lin"

GABAPENTIN (Neurontin)
"gab-uh-PEN-tin"

CARBAMAZEPINE (Tegretol)
"car-bah-MAZE-uh-peen"

Carbamazepine is a traditional anti-epileptic drug, the others are newer.

Poem: Gabapentin Ghazal

Gabapentin – nerves will dull,
And calm the neuropathic pain today,

Patients ask how the drug works, they mull,
Block transmitters that in the brain today?

To the seizure's foci the drug cries, "all stop full,"
The neural impulse, slow the nerve train today,

The restless leg syndrome's push and pull,
Appendages stop their dance refrain today,

Guerra the pharmacist will cull,
Epileptic prescriptions written not in vain today.

Gabapentin Ghazal. A ghazal is a poetic form that I loosely followed. There is rhyme between the last word of the first line of each couplet and the second to last word in each second line of the couplet. Traditionally a poet puts their name in the second to last line. There is supposed to be a big transition from one couplet to the next, I just used various indications for gabapentin.

Antiepileptics (cont'd)

Brand names

TOPAMAX uses five letters from **top**iram**a**te, seizures it helps to abate.
"TOE-puh-max"

TRILEPTAL tries to prevents epi**lept**ic attacks.
"try-LEP-tall"

Generic names

TOPIRAMATE (Topamax)
"tope-EAR-uh-mate"

OXCARBAZEPINE (Trileptal)
"ox-car-BAZ-eh-peen"

Both are newer antiepileptics.

Drugs for Alzheimer's

ARICEPT improves per**cept**ion and **A**lzheimer's patients' recollection.
"ERR-eh-sept"

DONEPEZIL (Aricept)
"Doe-NEP-eh-zill"

Poem: Idiopathic

(a disease of unknown cause)
Someone crept through her
streamers, slicing them, building
a petrified forest of the rest.

Now, the funerals walk single file,
cut familiar strangers speaking in
echoes she ought to understand.

The long white coat refuses to say,
"I don't know", for that would deliver
hope, breaking her Hippocratic oath

implying someone might know.
Instead, she charts an adjective
that politely says, "no one knows."

He is an unlucky dog, salty – now bitter,
tasting each blue-penciled tendril. Alone
with her, he pleads not for her to be

spared, but that he might fly with her,
into a transparent pane, as Fischer or Lillian
might, breaking their necks together – perfectly quick.

Idiopathic After 50 years, some people are not meant to live

apart from each other. Alzheimer's is not only difficult on the

patient, but also on the caregiver. Fischer and Lillian are

species of lovebirds.

Drugs for Parkinson's

Brand names

SINEMET works **syn**ergistically to help Parkinson's patients' tremors cease.
"SIN-uh-met"

ELDEPRYL helps with Parkinson's disease, a condition more prevalent in the **elderly** we see.
"EL-duh-pril"

MIRAPEX takes the *mi* and *pex* from pramipexole, to help Parkinson's patients that might be young or old.
"MEER-uh-pecks"

Generic names

LEVODOPA/CARBIDOPA (Sinemet)
"LEE-vo-doe-pa CAR-bid-oh-pa"

SELEGILINE (Eldepryl)
"se-LEDGE-eh-lean"

PRAMIPEXOLE (Mirapex)
"pram-eh-PEX-ole"

Vertigo/motion sickness

Brand names

ANTIVERT an **anti-vertigo** drug to help get rid of the dizziness bug.
"ANT-e-vert"

TRANSDERM-SCOP is a **trans**dermal form of **scop**olamine, for motion sickness on Caribbean cruising.
"trans-DERM SCOPE"

Generic names

MECLIZINE (Antivert)
"MECK-luh-zeen"

SCOPOLAMINE (Transderm-Scop)
"sco-POL-uh-mean"

Muscle relaxation

Brand names

DANTRIUM uses the five letters of **dantr**olene, to relax spasms that are more than annoying.
"DAN-tree-um"

FLEXERIL a muscle relaxer that improves **flexibility**.
"FLEX-er-ill"

LIORESAL **li**ghtens, **re**laxes **spin**al spasticity.
"Lee-OR-is-Al"

SKELAXIN **relax**es **skel**etal muscle.
"SKELL-ax-in"

Generic names

DANTROLENE (Dantrium)
"DAN-tro-lean"

CYCLOBENZAPRINE (Flexeril)
"sigh-clo-BENDS-uh-preen"

BACLOFEN (Liorisal)
"BACK-low-fen"

METAXOLONE (Skelaxin)
"met-AX-uh-lone"

Nervous system drug practice

Classify these drugs by placing the corresponding drug class letter next to each medication:

1. Alprazolam
2. Amitryptiline
3. Atomoxetine
4. Citalopram
5. Dexmethylphenidate
6. Divalproex
7. Haloperidol
8. Isocarboxazid
9. Levodopa/carbidopa
10. Zolpidem

Nervous System Drug Classes:

A. Sedative-hypnotic
B. Antidepressant: SSRI
C. Antidepressant: TCA
D. Antidepressant: MAOI
E. Benzodiazepine
F. ADHD drug/stimulant
G. ADHD drug/non-stimulant
H. First-generation anti-psychotic
I. Traditional antiepileptic
J. Anti-Parkinson's

CHAPTER 6 – CARDIOLOGY

The four classes of diuretics

There are four generally accepted classes of diuretic:

Osmotic – These increase the osmolarity of blood, why they are named that way, and can be used to reduce intracranial pressure. An example is **mannitol (Osmitrol)**.

Loop – These are named after the part of the nephron that the drug works in, the Loop of Henle, and produce significant dieresis. An example is **furosemide (Lasix)**.

Thiazide – These are named after the suffix of the generic drug name such as **hydrochlorothiazide (Hydrodiuril)**. They don't produce as much dieresis as loop diuretics, but are excellent for hypertension.

Potassium sparing – These drugs will keep potassium in the body which is very important as loop and thiazide diuretics excrete potassium. They do not produce much diuresis. An example is **spironolactone (Aldactone)**.

Diuretics

ALDACTONE is spironol**actone**.
"Al-DAK-tone"

BUMEX is short for the loop diuretic **bume**tanide.
"BYOU-mex"

HYDRODIURIL is combined from **diuretic** and **hydro**chlorothiazide.
"high-droe-DIE-yer-ill"

LASIX is a loop diuretic that **lasts six** hours.
"LAY-six"

Generic names

SPIRONOLACTONE (Aldactone) is potassium sparing and can cause gynecomastic pairing.

"spur-oh-no-LACK-tone"

BUMETANIDE (Bumex)
"byou-MET-uh-nide"

HYDROCHLOROTHIAZIDE (Hydrodiuril)
"High-droe-klor-oh-THIGH-uh-zide"

FUROSEMIDE (Lasix)
"fur-OH-seh-mide"

Aldactone is a potassium-sparing diuretic, HCTZ a thiazide diuretic, and the other two are loop diuretics.

Diuretics (cont'd)

Brand name

OSMITROL is mannit**ol**, an **osm**otic diuretic.
"OZ-meh-trawl"

Generic name
MANNITOL (Osmitrol)
"MAN-eh-tall"

Poem: Nephron's Turns (for the Worse)

Mannitol saved Bruce,
     Before his proximal fate,

Furosemide,
     Looped Carter as a knave,

HCTZ,
     Distraught, lost his K,

Triamterene,
     Collects spare change.

Nephron's Turns (for the Worse). Mannitol was used when Bruce Lee had swelling in his brain, Carter from *ER* got beat up (verbally) as a medical resident on the diuretic furosemide, HCTZ causes the body to lose potassium (K), and triamterene is a potassium-*spar*ing diuretic. The drug order follows a nephron from the proximal convoluted tubule to collecting duct.

Poem: Cat Eye on Yesterday Morning's Breakfast

Raised and extended like a slim furry sail,
She sniffs, stares into the white garbage pail,

The cat eye on
In salted bacon,
Like Natrium, *is a positive one.*

In sliced banana,
Like Kalium, *is a positive one, too.*

In soured milk,
Like Calcium, *is a positive two.*

In solid oats,
Like Magnesium, *is a positive two, too.*

Disenchanted,
she skulks away,
to spot her
paw in the
pool,
Now she has,
an eye on,
green chloride.

What the cat keeps an eye on, *it's a negative one.*

Cat Eye On Yesterday Morning's Breakfast. The *cat eye on* is a
play on *cation*, a positively charged electrolyte: *sodium*
(natrium in Latin), *potassium* (kalium in Latin), *calcium* (calx
in Latin), and *magnesium* and an eye on (anion) – *chloride.*

Understanding the alpha's and beta's

Confusion about alpha and beta adrenergic blockers (antagonists) comes from seeing receptor and neurotransmitter names instead of seeing therapeutic classes. Adrenergic means works like adrenaline (**epinephrine**) so an adrenergic agonist works like adrenaline and an adrenergic antagonist works in the opposite way.

The prefix adren- refers to it being discovered in the adrenal glands. The adrenal glands are above (ad-) the kidneys (-renal) and secrete adrenaline (epinephrine). The suffix –ergic refers to the Greek for "works like." Instead of calling **metoprolol** (**Lopressor**) an antihypertensive, it is called a beta blocker. That is just the convention or how people say it. Instead of calling **doxazosin** (**Cardura**) an antihypertensive, it is called an alpha blocker. That could also be called a drug for benign prostatic hyperplasia.

We do this because **metoprolol** (**Lopressor**) can also be used to prevent migraines, treat dysrhythmias, treat heart failure, and off-label for performance anxiety. However, it does not do anything for benign prostatic hyperplasia (enlarged prostate) as an alpha blocker, a different drug, does.

Alpha blockers (for hypertension)

Brand names

CARDURA provides **dura**ble **card**iac relief of hypertension.
"CAR-dur-uh"

HYTRIN is a drug for **hy**pertens**ion** and has the same suffix as terazos**in**.
"HIGH-trin"

Generic names

DOX<u>AZOSIN</u> (Cardura)
"Docks-AZ-oh-sin"

TER<u>AZOSIN</u> (Hytrin)
"Ter-AZ-oh-sin"

Alpha agonist

Brand name

CATAPRES catabolizes (lowers) blood **pres**sure and starts with the same letter as the **c**lonidine as well.
"CAT-uh-press"

Generic name

CLONIDINE (Catapres)
"KLON-eh-dean"

Alpha blockers might end in -azosin.

Beta blockers

Brand names

COREG regulates **cor**onary function.
"CO-reg"

LOPRESSOR lowers blood **pressure.**
"low-PRESS-or"

TENORMIN normalizes hyper**ten**sion.
"TEN-or-min"

Generic names

CARVEDILOL (Coreg)
"car-VE-deh-lawl"

 METOPROLOL (Lopressor)
"meh-TOE-pruh-lawl"

ATENOLOL (Tenormin)
"uh-TEN-uh-lawl"

Beta blockers usually end in –olol or –lol. A Mnemonic tool: -olol and beta blockers (bb) both repeat letters.

The renin-angiotensin-aldosterone-system drugs

This system, the **RAAS**, is meant to control blood pressure and by defining a couple of words we can better understand how the drugs work.

Renin – The word come from renal for kidneys and this chemical changes angiotensinogen to angiotensin I.

Angiotensin I – A chemical that can be converted to **angiotensin II**, which is a potent vasoconstrictor (blood vessel constrictor) which increases blood pressure when our body needs it.

So an **angiotensin converting enzyme inhibitors (ACE inhibitors)** such as **lisinopril (Zestril)** stops the body from creating this potent vasoconstrictor easing up the blood vessels and reducing hypertension.

ARBs, or angiotensin II receptor blockers, such as **valsartan (Diovan)** work by blocking or inhibiting the connection between angiotensin II and the receptor that would cause vasoconstriction.

ACE Inhibitors (ACEI)

Brand names

ACCUPRIL is **accurate**, an **ace** reducing pressure rate.
"ACK-you-pril"

ALTACE is an **alt**ernate ace inhibitor.
"AL-tace"

CAPOTEN uses the first five letters of **capto**pril.
"KAP-oh-ten"

VASOTEC technically affects the **vas**culature.
"VA-zo-tech"

Generic names

QUINA<u>PRIL</u> (Accupril)
"QUINN-uh-pril"

RAMI<u>PRIL</u> (Altace)
"RAM-eh-pril"

CAPTO<u>PRIL</u> (Capoten)
"KAP-toe-pril"

ENALA<u>PRIL</u> (Vasotec)
"eh-NAL-uh-pril"

ACE inhibitors usually end in –pril.

ACE inhibitors (ACEI) (cont'd)

Brand names

ZESTRIL has the suffix –**ril**, like the ACE inhibitor lisino**pril**.
"ZES-tril"

Generic names

LISINOPRIL (Zestril) thrills an overworked heart, blocking angiotensin II from getting a start.
"lie-SIN-oh-pril"

ACE inhibitors usually end in –pril.

Angiotensin II receptor blockers (ARBs)

Brand names

COZAAR is a **co**ronary **a**ngiotensin II **r**eceptor **a**ntagonist, (ARA) with the letters in bit of a twist.
 "CO-tsar"

DIOVAN has three of the letters of **v**als**a**rta**n**.
"DYE-oh-van"

Generic names

LO<u>SAR</u>TAN (Cozaar)
"low-SAR-tan"

VAL<u>SARTA</u>N (Diovan)
"val-SAR-tan"

ARBs usually end in –sartan. ACEIs with –pril.

D'artagnan the musketeer has to be *-sartan* with the b*ARB* of his blade, otherwise he's not be an *ACE* in A-*pril* I'm afraid.

Calcium channel blockers (CCBs)

Brand names

CALAN is a **cal**cium ch**an**nel blocker.
"KALE-en"

CARDIZEM is the **card**iac drug dil**tiazem**.
"CAR-deh-zem"

NORVASC normalizes the **vasc**ulature.
"NOR-vasc"

PROCARDIA promotes **cardia**c health.
"pro-CARD-e-uh"

Generic names

VERAPAMIL (Calan) **Vera** and **Pam** are **il**(l)and need this calcium blocking cardiac pill
"ver-APP-uh-mill"

DILTIAZEM (Cardizem)
"dill-TIE-uh-zem"

AMLO<u>DIPINE</u> (Norvasc)
"am-LOW-duh-peen"

NIFE<u>DIPINE</u> (Procardia)
"nigh-FED-eh-peen"

Verapamil and diltiazem significantly affect the heart, amlodipine and nifedipine, which have the suffix –dipine, do not.

Poem: The Hypertensive Abecedarian

(to be read as quickly as the fine print in a drug commercial)

Al asked his aged doc about his abnormally high blood
pressure to which the doctor ardently and adamantly refused to
prescribe an alpha-blocker or ACE inhibitor, instead
prescribing atenolol, a
Beta 1 selective blocker; which might avoid bronchospasm,
while bisoprolol might have done just fine too, or even a
Calcium channel blocker (CCB) can work; captopril the ACE
inhibitor, carvedilol, the beta-blocker with alpha-blocking
activity, and
Diltiazem, the non-dihydropyridine CCB, definitely are
dependable alternates,
Enalapril, even,
Fosinopril, ACE inhibitors both, formed functionally better
offerings than,
Guanfacine, which gradually gets weaned off of because of
rebound
Hypertension. Would HCTZ, hydrochlorothiazide, historically
the first-line therapy help?
Irbisartan, would be fine indeed, an angiotensin-two -receptor-
antagonist (ARB), but with HCTZ, I'm
Just worried about your
Kalium, your potassium levels, you know,
Lisinopril, the ACE inhibitor, might cause long lagging
coughs,
Metoprolol, a selective beta-blocker might make sense
therapeutically, but many confuse tartrate and succinate salt
dosing, immediate versus extended release, man, it's not like
you have angina, where you
Need nitroglycerin, no let's not use

Olmesartan, or any other ARB, or
Propranolol, non-selective possibility, putting bronchi in potential peril,
Quinapril and
Ramipril, ACE inhibitors both,
Sotalol,
Timolol, beta blockers both, too many me-too choices,
Understand, I could name umpteen high blood pressure drugs,
Valsartan, the ARB, Verapamil the CCB,
Warfarin, if things get clogged, but for right now be wary of
Xanthines, methylxanthines, I mean, like caffeine,
You'll be younger for a bit of yoga then yell for me in four weeks when we'll re-evaluate and consider
Zofenopril.

The Hypertensive Abecedarian. I was poking fun at the number of choices that we have with some of the anti-hypertensive classes and how confusing it can become because of the number of me-too drugs. I enjoy reading this at "fine print" pace to my students. As an exercise you can circle the beta-blockers that end in *–olol*, the ACE inhibitors ending in *–pril*, and the ARBs ending in *–sartan*.

Antihyperlipidemics (cholesterol-lowering drugs)

Brand names

LIPITOR is a **lip**id gladia**tor**.
"LIP-eh-tore"

LOPID lowers the li**pid** triglyceride.
"LOW-pid"

ZETIA uses letters from **ezeti**mibe, so cholesterol doesn't rise.
"ZET-e-uh"

ZOCOR reduces lipids moving through the **cor**onary arteries.
"ZO-cor"

Generic names

ATORV**ASTATIN** (Lipitor)
"uh-TOUR-va-stat-in"

GEMFIBROZIL (Lopid)
"gem-FIE-bro-zil"

EZETIMIBE (Zetia)
"eh-ZET-eh-mibe"

SIMV**ASTATIN** (Zocor)
"SIM-va-stat-in"

HMG-CoA reductase inhibitors are abbreviated statins, though the correct suffix is –vastatin.

Anticoagulant/antiplatelet

Brand names

COUMADIN is an anti-**co**agulant much like aspi**rin**.
"KOO-ma-din"

HEPARIN is an excellent anticoagulant by far. Its name
comes from the Greek for liver –**hepar**.
"HEP-uh-rin"

LOVENOX is a **low** molecular weight heparin for deep **vein**
thrombosis prevention.
"LOW-ven-ox"

PLAVIX vexes platelets and keeps the blood thin.
"PLA-vix"

Generic names

WARFARIN (Coumadin)
"WAR-fa-rin"

HEPARIN
"HEP-uh-rin"

ENOXAPARIN (Lovenox)
"e-knocks-uh-PEAR-in"

CLOPIDOGREL (Plavix)
"klo-PID-oh-grel"

Warfarin, heparin, and enoxaparin are considered
anticoagulants. Clopidogrel and aspirin are antiplatelet
medications.

Song: Cardiode to Joy (sung to Beethoven's Ode to Joy)

Note: 15 beats in the first 4 lines

o-l-o-l-p-r-i-l-and-s-a-r-t-a-n

be-ta-block-er-ace-in-hib-i-tor-and-ARBs-suff-ix-end

as-pir-in-and-clo-pid-o-grel-both-block-plate-lets-round-a-stent

war-fa-rin-and-hep-a-rin-are-both-an-ti-co-ag-u-lants

stat-ins-low-er-chol-est-ter-ol

dig-keeps-your-heart-from-fail-in

ver-a-pa-mil-and-am-lo-di-pine

both-block-cal-cium-chan-nels

Antidysrhythmics

Brand names

CORDARONE combines **cor**onary and amio**darone** to make a good antidysrhythmic pairing.
"CORE-duh-rone"

LANOXIN uses the suffix from dig**oxin,** to keep your heartbeat rockin'.
"la-KNOCKS-in"

XYLOCAINE is lid**ocaine**, also used to stop pain.
"ZIE-low-cane"

Generic names

AMIODARONE (Cordarone)
"am-e-OH-duh-rone"

 DIGOXIN (Lanoxin)
"di-JOCKS-in"

LIDOCAINE (Xylocaine)
"lie-DOE-cane"

Digoxin is in a class of drugs known as the cardiac glycosides.

Poem: Pulling the Lion's Tooth

I enjoy taking
a half-foot
of forked iron
cracking
the connection
between
the yellow dendrite's
axonal root
clinging
to the wall socket

The last spark
jumping, crying
across
the polarized air.

Pulling the Lion's Tooth. Dandelion is French for a lion's tooth and while I was pulling them I thought about how I was pulling the plug on its life. My wife was on bed rest the year before, so it pulled more than six buckets of dandelions to clear our quarter-acre yard. The great pleasure I got was more from being done with the task for this year. The flower looked like a neuronal dendrite to me and the root an axon, two structures critical in electrical and signal impulse transmission.

Cardiovascular drug practice

Classify these drugs by placing the corresponding drug class letter next to each medication:

1. Atorvastatin
2. Clopidogrel
3. Enalapril
4. Enoxaparin
5. Furosemide
6. Hydrochlorothiazide
7. Losartan
8. Metoprolol
9. Nifedipine
10. Spironolactone

Cardiovascular drug classes:

A. Diuretic: Potassium sparing
B. Diuretic: Thiazide
C. Diuretic: Loop
D. Selective beta blocker
E. ACE inhibitor (ACEI)
F. Angiotensin receptor blocker (ARB)
G. Calcium channel blocker (CCB)
H. HMG Co-A reductase inhibitor
I. Anticoagulant
J. Antiplatelet

CHAPTER 7 – ENDOCRINE

Diabetes and insulin

Diabetes Mellitus is an excess of blood sugar. There are three types: type I which sometimes is referred to as juvenile onset diabetes, type II, which can be referred to as "adult-onset diabetes" and gestational diabetes, a condition where pregnant women (not previously diabetic) become diabetic. Depending on the condition there are different drugs that can help lower blood sugar from tablets like **metformin (Glucophage)**, to insulin to other injectables.

Insulin for diabetes comes from the Latin word insula, which means island. The islets of Langerhans have cells to produce insulin (Beta cells) and to tell the body to raise blood glucose levels with glucagon (Alpha cells). There are four major classes of insulin substitute used in treatment: *rapid acting* which starts working in about 15 minutes and lasts about 4 hours like **insulin lispro (Humalog),** *slower acting* works in about 30 minutes and last about 6 to 8 hours like **regular insulin (Humulin R)**, *intermediate duration* like **NPH insulin (Humulin N)** which starts working in an hour or two and lasts one-half to most of the day and *long duration* **insulin glargine (Lantus)** which starts working in about an hour and lasts 24 hours.

Diabetes

Brand names

ACTOS acts on **glucose.**
"ACK-toes"

AVANDIA is an **advan**ced **dia**betic drug.
"uh-van-DEE-uh"

DIABETA is for **dia**betics, working on the **beta** cells, from which insulin is let out.
"die-uh-BAY-ta"

 GLUCAGEN generates **gluc**ose when a patient is hypoglycemic. Use it when the glucose is gone.
"glue-ca-JEN"

Generic names

PIOGLITAZONE (Actos)
"pie-oh-GLIT-uh-zone"

ROSIGLITAZONE (Avandia)
"rose-eh-GLIT-uh-zone"

GLYBURIDE (Diabeta)
"gly-byou-ride"

GLUCAGON (GlucaGen)
"GLUE-ca-gone"

Note: Glucagon is not for someone who is diabetic with high blood sugar; rather, for someone whose sugar is too low.

Diabetes (cont'd)

Brand names

GLUCOPHAGE phages, or eats **glucose**, if you **met four men** on glucophage, they are diabetic.
"GLUE-co-fage"

GLUCOTROL controls blood **glucose** in diabetics.
"GLUE-co-trawl"

HUMULIN is **hum**an ins**ulin**.
"HUE-myou-lin"

Generic names

METFORMIN (Glucophage)
"met-FOUR-men"

GLIPIZIDE (Glucotrol)
"GLIP-eh-zide"

INSULIN (Humulin)
"IN-su-lin"

Thyroid hormones

Thyroid hormone 1) stimulates the heart 2) stimulates metabolism 3) helps with growth. A hyperthyroid patient's body is using energy too quickly and needs a medication such as **propylthiouracil (PTU)** to reduce the effects of thyroid hormone. Hypothyroid patients need extra thyroid hormone, such as **levothyroxine (Synthroid)** to replace what they are missing.

Drugs for hypothyroidism

Brand names

SYNTHROID is a **synthetic thyroid** replacement, once in the morning, with no food you take it.
"SIN-throyd"

Generic names

LEVOTHYROXINE (Synthroid)
"Lee-vo-thigh-ROCKS-een"

Drugs for hyperthyroidism

Brand name

PTU is the acronym for **p**ropyl**t**hio**u**racil, a thyroid hormone blocking pill.
"PEA-tee-you"

Generic name

PROPYLTHIOURACIL (PTU)
"PRO-pill-thigh-oh-your-uh-sill"

Endocrine drug practice

Classify these drugs by placing the corresponding drug class letter next to each medication:

1. Glipizide
2. Glucagon
3. Glyburide
4. Insulin glargine
5. Levothyroxine
6. Metformin
7. Pioglitazone
8. PTU
9. Regular insulin
10. Rosiglitazone

Endocrine system drug classes:

A. Anti-diabetic
B. Long duration insulin
C. Slower acting insulin
D. For hypoglycemia
E. For hypothyroidism
F. For hyperthyroidism

CHAPTER 8 – RENAL/REPRODUCTIVE

Incontinence, impotence, urinary retention, BPH

Frequently the words incontinence, impotence, urinary retention and benign prostatic hyperplasia are confused:

Incontinence is the inability to retain urine.

Impotence is the inability to maintain an erection.

Urinary retention is a difficulty in urination.

BPH is an acronym for *benign prostatic hyperplasia* which is a non-cancerous growth of the prostate.

Alpha blockers can be used for hypertension, but they also make effective drugs for BPH.

Incontinence

Brand names

DETROL helps **control** the **detrusor** muscle keeping urine in.
"deh-TRAWL"

DITROPAN ropes and shuts down the **detrusor** muscle.
"DIH-trow-pan"

Generic names

TOLTERODINE (Detrol)
"toll-TER-oh-dean"

OXYBUTYNIN (Ditropan)
"ox-e-BYOU-tin-in"

Urinary retention

Brand names

URECHOLINE controls **ur**ine through anti**choline**rgic effects.
"your-eh-CO-lean"

Generic names

BETHANECHOL (Urecholine)
"beth-ANN-uh-call"

Impotence (erectile dysfunction)

Brand names

CIALIS lasts the weekend.
"see-AL-is"

LEVITRA levitates and **raises**.
"le-VEE-truh"

VIAGRA brings **vi**able **gr**owth.
"vie-AG-rah"

Generic names

TAD<u>ALAFIL</u> (Cialis)
"ta-DA-la-fill"

VAR<u>DENAFIL</u> (Levitra)
"var-DEN-uh-fill"

SIL<u>DENAFIL</u> (Viagra)
"sill-DEN-uh-fill"

PED5 inhibitors for erectile dysfunction end in -denafil, -alafil

Poem: Sexting with Snail Mail Part I

When the blue diamond-shaped pill
emerged a man could again,
but how?

He'd long been out of the game.

He might go to his trusted advisors –
grandchildren – certainly not his kids.

(Because who wants to think
about their dad doing it?)

He might ask, "How do I?"

The grandchildren say proudly,
whether they did or didn't,
"We *sext* each other."

A taste of silence.

"You've never heard of *sexting*?"

He nods to an olive-green
rotary phone.

"Granddad, what did you used to do?"

Poem: Sexting with Snail Mail Part II

He would sit alone with her picture,

> a blank page waiting,
> a blank page watching,
> a blank page wanting,

The pen, the picture, the page,
The pen, the picture,
The picture,

His lexis looped his pen to,

Cull her nape, with a slow spiral e
Stroke her hair, with an unfinished r
Cup her breast, with the turn of a t
Warm her navel, with an upswept l
Cradle her back, with a firm k
Slide to her thigh, with a sharp downward h

Pulling it all off, in
One fluid motion.

Sexting with Snail Mail Parts I and II. I just put myself in the place of someone who had become impotent and came back from the pharmacy with Viagra. I wondered what it would be like to get back in the dating game at an older age.

Alpha blockers (for BPH)

Brand names

CARDURA provides **dura**ble **card**iac relief of hypertension.
"CAR-dur-uh"

FLOMAX allows for **max**imum urinary **flow**.
"FLOW-Max"

HYTRIN is a drug for **hy**pertens**ion** and has the same suffix as
terazos**in**.
"HIGH-trin"

Generic names

DOX<u>AZOSIN</u> (Cardura)
"Docks-AZ-oh-sin"

TAMSULOSIN (Flomax)
"tam-SUE-low-sin"

TER<u>AZOSIN</u> (Hytrin)
"Ter-AZ-oh-sin"

Other drugs for BPH

PROSCAR is good for **pros**tate **car**e.
"pro-SCAR"

FINASTERIDE (Proscar)
"fin-AS-ter-ide"

Alpha blockers use the –azosin suffix.

Reproductive and renal drug practice

Classify these drugs by placing the corresponding drug class letter next to each medication:

1. Bethanechol
2. Doxazosin
3. Finasteride
4. Oxybutynin
5. Sildenafil
6. Tadalafil
7. Tamsulosin
8. Terazosin
9. Tolterodine
10. Vardenafil

Reproductive and renal system drug classes:

A. Incontinence
B. Urinary Retention
C. Impotence
D. Alpha blocker for BPH
E. Other drug for BPH

CHAPTER 9 – MISCELLANEOUS DRUGS

Miscellaneous drugs I

Brand names

CORTEF has the root **cort** from the steroid hydro**cort**isone.
"core-TEF"

EPIPEN can save an anaphylactic patient from a **pen**icillin allergy with an **epi**nephrine **pen**.
"EP-e-pen"

ISOPTO ATROPINE's from the plant *atropa belladonna*.
Bella donna, pretty woman with **dilated** pupils.
"EYE-sop-toe AT-row-peen"

K-DUR - the chemical symbol for Potassium, **K**, in Latin is **Kalium** and **Dur**- short for long duration.
"KAY-dur"

Generic names

HYDROCORTISONE (Cortef)
"high-dro-CORE-'tis-own"

EPINEPHRINE (EpiPen)
"eh-pee-NEF-rin"

ATROPINE (Isopto-Atropine)
"AT-row-peen"

POTASSIUM CHLORIDE (K-Dur)
"po-TASS-e-um-KLOR-eyed"

Miscellaneous drugs II

Brand names

KETALAR is the anesthetic **ket**amine.
"KET-uh-lar"

MUCOMYST is a **mucolytic** antidote for acetaminophen poisoning and uses the generic name's root acetyl**cyst**eine.
"MYOU-co-mist"

NARCAN is a **narc**otic (opioid receptor) antagonist so you **can** get stop the feelings that addict.
"NAR-can"

NITROGLYCERIN is converted to **nitric** oxide, a vasodilator your body abides.
"nigh-trow-GLI-sir-in"

Generic names

KETAMINE (Ketalar)
"KET-uh-mean"

ACETYLCYSTEINE (Mucomyst)
"uh-see-till-SIS-teen"

NALOXONE (Narcan)
"Nal-ox-own"

NITROGLYCERIN
"nigh-trow-GLI-sir-in"

Miscellaneous drugs III

Brand names

NOVOCAINE comes from the Latin for new, "novo" and the suffix of pro**caine**, to stop pain.
"NOV-oh-cane"

PROCRIT provides improved hemato**crit**.
"pro-CRIT"

PROPECIA provides hair for men with alo**pecia**.
"pro-PEE-Shu"

SUDAFED is short for **pseudo**ephedrine, a decongestant.
"Sue-duh-FED"

Generic names

PROCAINE (Novocaine)
"PRO-cane"

EPOETIN (Procrit)
"e-poe-E-tin"

FINASTERIDE (Propecia)
"fin-AS-ter-ide"

PSEUDOEPHEDRINE (Sudafed)
"Sue-doe-uh-FED-ran"

Miscellaneous drugs IV

Brand name

SANDIMMUNE was invented by **Sand**oz and suppresses the **immune** system.
"sand-im-MYOON"

Generic name

CYCLOSPORINE (Sandimmune)
"SIGH-clo-spore-een"

Chapter 10 – Prefixes and suffixes

Poem: Pharmacology Sonnet – From Suffix First

In farm uh call oh gee a student learns
It is to name a drug from suffix first
Of –pril or –lol or other clues will turn
The lost to lucid; brings a brand of thirst

For more a challenge will she ask in time
As forests fall and branches bend in awe
For tongues no longer twist as words do shine
Such mastered breath so perfect without flaw

A doctor asks in hushed and gentle tones
How best to pronounce drugs to save a life
For wise patients will plead or sure bemoan
MD replete with poor syntax this night

Oh she then tells him not to fear today
Always the nurse is there to make the save

From Suffix First – A sonnet I use to help my students learn about the value of suffixes in grouping some drug classes together. Follows a traditional abab, cdcd, efef gg sonnet form. This outlines a nurse who, more familiar with the drug, helps a doctor avoid embarrassment in front of a patient. This happens sometimes around medical residents' first day on the job – July 1st.

Common suffixes (alphabetical)

-azole – Antifungal [-prazole will usually be a PPI]
-cillin – Penicillin antibiotic
-cycline – Tetracycline antibiotic
-denafil, -dalafil – PED5 inhibitors for erectile dysfunction
-dipine – Calcium channel blocker [some, not verapamil, diltiazem]
-dronate – Bisphosphonate for osteoporosis
-floxacin – Fluoroquinolone antibiotic
-olol, -lol – Beta blocker [avoid confusion with similar –terol]
-mab – monoclonal antibody
-micin, mycin – Aminoglycoside antibiotic [not -thromycin]
-parin – Anticoagulant
-prazole – PPI – acidic GI conditions [-azole alone is not enough]
-pril – ACEI angiotensin converting enzyme inhibitor (ACEI)
-sartan – Angiotensin II receptor blocker (ARB)
-sone – Corticosteroid for inflammation
-terol – Bronchodilator for asthma [confusion with –olol –lol]
-tidine – H_2 Blocker – acidic GI conditions
-thromycin – Macrolide antibiotic
-triptan – Serotonin receptor agonist (migraines)
-vastatin – HMG Co-A reductase inhibitors ("statins")
                [Caution: nystatin is an antifungal]
-vir – Antiviral
-zosin, -osin – Alpha-blocker for BPH or hypertension
-zepam, -zolam – Benzodiazepine for anxiety, sleep

Common prefixes (alphabetical)

Cef-, ceph – Cephalosporin antibiotic
Sulfa – Sulfa antibiotic

Suffixes and prefixes sorted by physiologic system

Chapter 1 – GI

-prazole – PPI – acidic GI conditions [confused with -azole]
-tidine H_2 blocker – acidic GI conditions

Chapter 2 – Musculoskeletal

-dronate – Bisphosphonate for osteoporosis
-mab – monoclonal antibody

Chapter 3 – Respiratory

-terol – Bronchodilator for asthma [confusion with –olol, –lol]
-sone – Corticosteroid for inflammation

Chapter 4 – Immune

-azole – Antifungal [don't confuse with prazole]
-cillin – Penicillin antibiotic
-cycline – Tetracycline antibiotic
-floxacin – Fluoroquinolone antibiotic
-micin, mycin – Aminoglycoside antibiotic [not -thromycin]
-thromycin – Macrolide antibiotic
-vir – Antiviral

Sulfa – Sulfa antibiotic.
Cef-, ceph – Cephalosporin antibiotic

Chapter 5 – Nervous

-triptan – Serotonin receptor agonist – (migraines)
-zepam, -zolam – Benzodiazepine for anxiety, sleep

Chapter 6 – Cardiology

-dipine – Calcium channel blocker [*some* not verapamil, diltiazem)

-olol, -lol – Beta blocker [avoid confusion with –terol]

-parin – Anticoagulant

-pril – Angiotensin converting enzyme inhibitor (ACEI)

-sartan – Antiotensin II receptor blocker (ARB)

-vastatin – HMG Co-A reductase inhibitors ("statins")
                    [Caution: nystatin is an antifungal]

-zosin, -osin – Alpha blocker for BPH or hypertension

Chapter 8 Renal/Reproductive

-denafil, -dalafil – PED5 inhibitors for erectile dysfunction

Commonly confused suffixes – Practice questions

On the next two pages are 16 commonly confused suffixes. When –azole is in the suffix, it might be an antifungal, but if the suffix is –prazole then it is more likely a proton pump inhibitor (PPI) or might be aripiprazole, a drug for schizophrenia.

By completing these eight pairs you can be more aware of possible misinterpretations of certain drug suffixes which are either spelled similarly or have parts of other suffixes in them.

1. Use either azithromycin or gentamicin

_____ is a macrolide antibiotic.
_____ is an aminoglycoside antibiotic.

Hint:
The longer suffix is the macrolide.
The shorter suffix is the aminoglycoside.

2. Use either omeprazole or fluconazole.

_____is an antifungal.
_____is a proton pump inhibitor.

Hint:
The longer suffix is the PPI.
The shorter suffix is the antifungal.

3. Use either nystatin or atorvastatin.

_____is an antifungal.
_____is a cholesterol medication.

Hint:
The longer suffix is the drug for cholesterol.
The shorter suffix is the antifungal.

4. Use either albuterol or metoprolol.

_____is an asthma medication.
_____is a drug for hypertension.

Hint:
The suffix –olol and –lol are for beta blockers.
The suffix –terol is for bronchodilators.

5. Use either amlodipine or ranitidine.

_____ is a stomach medicine.
_____ is a medication for blood pressure.

Hint:
The suffix –dipine is a calcium channel blocker?
The suffix –tidine is an H$_2$ blocker?

6. Use either tamsulosin or prednisone.

_____is for inflammatory conditions.
_____is for BPH.

Hint:
The –osin is for prostate.
The –sone is for a steroid.

7. Use either sumatriptan or simvastatin.

_____is a cholesterol drug.
_____is for migraines.

Hint:
One trips up headaches?
Statins are for cholesterol?

8. Use either enoxaparin or enalapril.

_____is an ACE inhibitor.
_____is an anticoagulant.

Hint:
The one like "heparin" is the anticoagulant.
The –pril suffix indicates a drug for hypertension.

Chapter 11 – Commonly confused drug names.

Health practitioners confuse drug names because they look very similar, but there is a little more to it than that.

It's pssioble to raed tihs sneetcne bceuase a preosn raeds a wolhe wrod nad nto jsut each lteter so as lnog sa teh frist adn lsat lteter aer crrocet it is sitll lgebile.

It's possible to read this sentence because a person reads a whole word and not just each letter so as long as the first and last letter are correct it is still legible.

That causes problems with drug names that have many of the same letters in them. So it is important to practice paying very close attention to drug names by having challenges that make you slow down and read each letter, rather than every word.

Use what you learned from the brand name drug mnemonics and generic prefixes and suffixes to get the right answer. If you get stuck, there is a hint below. I have capitalized both drug names so as not to give it away, however, it is proper to capitalize a brand name and use lower case for a generic name.

1. Use either Axert or Antivert.

_____ is a migraine medicine.
_____ is a medication that helps dizziness.

Hint:
*Which **ax's** out a headache that hurts?*
*Which is an anti-**vertigo** drug?*

2. Use either Aricept or Aciphex.

_____is an alzheimer's medication.
_____is a proton pump inhibitor.

Hint:
*Which helps improver **perception**?*
*Which **affects** the **pH** and acid?*

3. Use either Advair or Advicor.

_____is a combination asthma medication.
_____is a combination cholesterol medication.

Hint:
*Which adds two drugs to help improve **airflow**?*
*Which helps protect a person's **coronary** arteries?*

4. Use either Allegra or Viagra.

_____is an allergy medicine.
_____is an erectile dysfunction medicine.

Hint:
*Which adds drugs rearranges the word **allergy**?*
*Which makes something **viable** and allows it to **grow**?*

5. Use either Atacand or Antacid.

_____ is a stomach medicine.
_____ is a medication for blood pressure.

Hint:
*Which is an **anti-acid**?*
*Which has the prefix of a –**sartan** blood pressure medicine?*

6. Use either Asacol or Os-Cal.

_____is for bowel conditions.
_____is a calcium supplement.

Hint:
*Which helps **assuage a colon**?*
*Which affects **osseous** (bone) tissue?*

7. Use either Benadryl or Benazepril.

_____is an antihistamine.
_____is an ACE inhibitor.

Hint:
Which adds drys up mucous?
What drug class does the –pril suffix signify?

8. Use either Captopril or Carvedilol.

_____is an ACE inhibitor.
_____is a beta blocker.

Hint:
Which drug class does the -pril suffix signify?
Which drug class does the –olol or –lol suffix signify?

9. Use either Celexa or Celebrex.

_____ is a non-steroidal anti-inflammatory drug
_____ is an antidepressant.

Hint:
*Which **relaxes** someone?*
*Which **celebrates** relief from pain?*

10. Use either Colace or Cozaar.

_____is a stool softener.
_____is a blood pressure medication.

Hint:
*Which makes your **colon race**?*
*Which affects the **RAAS**?*

11. Use either Diabeta or Zebeta.

_____is a blood pressure medication.
_____is a diabetic medication.

Hint:
*Which has the root for a **diabetic**?*
*Which is "**ze**" **beta** blocker?*

12. Use either Flonase or Flovent.

_____is for allergic rhinitis.
_____is for asthma.

Hint:
Which has the prefix for nasal?
Which helps ventilate an asthmatic?

13. Use either Atorvastatin or Nystatin.

_____ is a cholesterol-lowering medicine.
_____ is an antifungal.

Hint:
Which does the suffix –vastatin signify?
Which is a generic for Mycostatin?

14. Use either Lanoxin or Levothyroxine.

_____is for thyroid replacement.
_____is to strengthen cardiac contraction.

Hint:
*Which helps comes from the **digitalis** plant?*
*Which affects **thyroid**?*

15. Use either Lariam or Levaquin.

_____is an antibiotic for infection.
_____is for malaria prevention.

Hint:
*Which has most of the word **malaria** jumbled?*
*What has the **fluoroquinolone** antibiotic root?*

16. Use either Lasix or Luvox.

_____is an antidepressant.
_____is a diuretic.

Hint:
*Which is a diuretic that **lasts six** hours?*
*Which is a root in the generic name **fluvoxamine**?*

17. Use either Lopressor or Lyrica.

_____ is a beta blocker for blood pressure.
_____ is a medicine to relieve neuropathic pain.

Hint:
*Which makes you feel **lyrical** after becoming pain free?*
*Which is to **lower** blood **pressure**?*

18. Use either Lotronex or Protonix.

_____is a medicine for irritable bowel syndrome.
_____is for acid reflux.

Hint:
*Which **nixes protons** reducing acid?*
*Which **lowers travel** time for diarrhea?*

19. Use either Lunesta or Neulasta.

_____is a hypnotic to help someone sleep.
_____is used to reduce the chance of infection.

Hint:
*Which puts you by the moon (**luna**) and helps you **rest**?*
*Which increases the **neutrophils**?*

20. Use either Metformin or Metronidazole.

_____is an antimicrobial.
_____is for diabetes.

Hint:
*Which drug would have **met four** diabetic **men**?*
*Which has the suffix –**azole** indicating possible antimicrobial?*

21. Use either Methergine or Brethine.

_____ is used to stop bleeding.
_____ is used for asthma.

Hint:
*Which helps with **breathing**?*
*Which helps with **mothering**?*

22. Use either Mirapex or Miralax.

_____is for constipation.
_____is for Parkinson's.

Hint:
*Which has a **laxative** effect?*
*Which is a brand name for **pramipexole**?*

23. Use either Neurontin or Motrin.

_____is a non-steroidal anti-inflammatory drug.
_____is for neuropathic pain.

Hint:
Which has the root of neuron?
Which better rhymes with aspirin, a non-steroidal?

24. Use either Noroxin or Neurontin.

_____is for seizures.
_____is an antibiotic.

Hint:
Which has part of the –floxacin suffix?
Which has the root for neuron?

25. Use either Oxycodone or Oxycontin.

_____ is long acting oxycodone .
_____ is short acting oxycodone.

Hint:
*Which has part of **continuous** in the name?*
*Which has **one** in the name?*

26. Use either Paxil or Plavix.

_____is a blood thinner.
_____is an antidepressant.

Hint:
*Which **vexes platelets**?*
*Which is the generic for the SSRI **paroxetine**?*

27. Use either Proscar or Provera.

_____is for BPH.
_____is used for women.

Hint:
*Which has **prostate** in the word?*
*Which has a **woman's name** in the word?*

28. Use either Restoril or Risperdal.

_____is an antipsychotic.
_____is a hypnotic for sleep.

Hint:
*Which has **rest** in the word?*
*Which is the brand name of **risperidone**?*

29. Use either Rozerem or Razadyne.

_____ is a sleep aid.
_____ is used for Alzheimer's.

Hint:
Which rhymes with **doze** has **REM** sleep in the word?
Which has the **az** sound of Alzheimer's?

30. Use either Zantac or Xanax.

_____is for acidic reflux.
_____is for anxiety.

Hint:
Which "**x's**" out **anxiety**?
Which is "**z**" **anti-acid**?

31. Use either Zebeta or Zetia.

_____is for hypertension.
_____is for hypercholesterolemia.

Hint:
Which is "**ze**" **beta**-blocker?
What is the brand name of **Ezetimibe**?

32. Use either aripiprazole or omeprazole.

_____is for schizophrenia.
_____is for acidic reflux.

Hint:
Which has the brand name **Abilify**, giving ability?
Which has the brand name **Prilosec**, protons low secretion?

Index and appendices

Answers to drug practice questions

Gastrointestinal drugs
1. A 2. B 3. E 4. B 5. C 6. F 7. A 8. G 9. C 10. D

Musculoskeletal drugs
1. B 2. I 3. F 4. J 5. H 6. C 7. D 8. A 9. G 10. E

Respiratory drugs
1. H 2. B 3. A 4. D 5. C 6. E 7. B 8. I 9. G 10. F

Immune system drugs
1. A 2. D 3. B 4. C 5. H 6. F 7. G 8. E 9. I 10. J

Nervous system drugs
1. E 2. C 3. G 4. B 5. F 6. I 7. H 8. D 9. J 10. A

Cardiovascular system drugs
1. H 2. J 3. E 4. I 5. C 6. B 7. F 8. D 9. G 10. A

Endocrine system drugs
1. A 2. D 3. A 4. B 5. E 6. A 7. A 8. F 9. C 10. A

Renal and reproductive system drugs
1. B 2. D 3. E 4. A 5. C 6. C 7. D 8. D 9. A 10. C

Answers to "Commonly confused suffixes"

1. Azithromycin is a macrolide antibiotic.
   Gentamicin is an aminoglycoside antibiotic.

2. Fluconazole is an antifungal.
   Omeprazole is a proton pump inhibitor.

3. Nystatin is an antifungal.
   Atorvastatin is a cholesterol medication.

4. Albuterol is an asthma medication.
   Metoprolol is a drug for hypertension.

5. Ranitidine is a stomach medicine.
   Amlodipine is a medication for blood pressure.

6. Prednisone is for inflammatory conditions.
   Tamsulosin is for BPH.

7. Simvastatin is a cholesterol drug.
   Sumatriptan is for migraines.

8. Enalapril is an ACE inhibitor.
   Enoxaparin is an anticoagulant.

Answers to "Commonly confused drug names"

1. Axert is a migraine medicine.
   Antivert is a medication that helps dizziness.

2. Aricept is an alzheimer's medication.
   Aciphex is a proton pump inhibitor.

3. Advair is a combination asthma medication.
   Advicor is a combination cholesterol medication.

4. Allegra is an allergy medicine.
   Viagra is an erectile dysfunction medicine.

5. Antacid is a stomach medicine.
   Atacand is a medication for blood pressure.

6. Asacol is for bowel conditions.
   Os-Cal is a calcium supplement.

7. Benadryl is an antihistamine.
   Benazepril is an ACE inhibitor.

8. Captopril is an ACE inhibitor.
   Carvedilol is a beta blocker.

9. Celebrex is a non-steroidal anti-inflammatory drug.
   Celexa is an antidepressant.

10. Colace is a stool softener.
    Cozaar is a blood pressure medication.

11. Zebeta is a blood pressure medication.
    Diabeta is a diabetic medication.

12. Flonase is for allergic rhinitis.
    Flovent is for asthma.

13. Atorvastatin is a cholesterol lowering medicine.
    Nystatin is an antifungal.

14. Levothyroxine is for thyroid replacement.
    Lanoxin is to strengthen cardiac contraction.

15. Levaquin is an antibiotic for infection.
    Lariam is for malaria prevention.

16. Luvox is an antidepressant.
    Lasix is a diuretic.

17. Lopressor is a beta blocker for blood pressure.
    Lyrica is a medicine to relieve neuropathic pain.

18. Lotronex is a medicine for irritable bowel syndrome.
    Protonix is for acid reflux.

19. Lunesta is a hypnotic to help someone sleep.
    Neulasta is used to reduce the chance of infection.

20. Metronidazole is an antimicrobial.
    Metformin is for diabetes.

21. Methergine is used to stop bleeding.
    Brethine is used for asthma.

22. Miralax is for constipation.
    Mirapex is for Parkinson's.

23. Motrin is a non-steroidal anti-inflammatory drug.
    Neurontin is for neuropathic pain.

24. Neurontin is for seizures.
    Neuroxin is an antibiotic.

25. Oxycontin is long acting oxycodone.
    Oxycodone is short acting oxycodone.

26. Plavix is a blood thinner.
    Paxil is an antidepressant.

27. Proscar is for BPH.
    Provera is used for women.

28. Risperdal is an antipsychotic.
    Restoril is a hypnotic for sleep.

29. Rozerem is a sleep aid.
    Razadyne is used for Alzheimer's.

30. Zantac is for acidic reflux.
    Xanax is for anxiety.

31. Zebeta is for hypertension.
    Zetia is for hypercholesterolemia.

32. Aripiprazole is for schizophrenia.
    Omeprazole is for acidic reflux.

Alphabetical listing of drug names

KEY

ALLCAPS ONLY = Brand name
ALLCAPS (Parenthesis) = GENERIC NAME (Brand name)

LIST OF DRUGS

ABILIFY
ABREVA
ACCUPRIL
ACETAMINOPHEN (Tylenol)
ACETYLCYSTEINE (Mucomyst)
ACIPHEX
ACTOS
ACYCLOVIR (Zovirax)
ADDERALL
ADVAIR
ALBUTEROL (ProAir)
ALDACTONE
ALENDRONATE (Fosamax)
ALEVE
ALLEGRA
ALLOPURINOL (Zyloprim)
ALMOTRIPTAN (Axert)
ALPRAZOLAM (Xanax)
ALTACE
ALUMINUM AND MAGNESIUM HYDROXIDE (Maalox)
AMBIEN
AMIKACIN (Amikin)
AMIKIN
AMIODARONE (Cordarone)
AMITRIPTYLINE (Elavil)

AMLODIPINE (Norvasc)
AMOXICILLIN (Amoxil)
AMOXICILLIN/CLAVULANATE (Augmentin)
AMOXIL
AMPHOTERICIN B (Fungizone)
ANTIVERT
ARICEPT
ARIPIPRAZOLE (Abilify)
ASACOL
ASPIRIN (Ecotrin)
ASPIRIN/ACETAMINOPHEN/CAFFEINE (Excedrin)
ATENOLOL (Tenormin)
ATIVAN
ATOMOXETINE (Strattera)
ATORVASTATIN (Lipitor)
ATROPINE (Isopto-Atropine)
ATROVENT
AUGMENTIN
AVANDIA
AVELOX
AXERT
AXID
AZITHROMYCIN (Zithromax)
AZMACORT
BACLOFEN (Liorisal)
BENADRYL
BENADRYL
BETHANECHOL (Urecholine)
BIAXIN
BISMUTH SUBSALICYLATE (Pepto-Bismol)
BONIVA
BRETHAIRE
BUMETANIDE (Bumex)
BUMEX
CALAN

CALCITONIN (Miacalcin)
CALCIUM CARBONATE (Os-Cal)
CALCIUM CARBONATE (Tums)
CALCIUM CARBONATE AND MAGNESIUM
HYDROXIDE (Rolaids)
CAPOTEN
CAPTOPRIL (Capoten)
CARBAMAZEPINE (Tegretol)
CARDIZEM
CARDURA
CARVEDILOL (Coreg)
CATAPRES
CEFEPIME (Maxipime)
CEFTAZIDIME (Fortaz)
CEFTRIAXONE (Rocephin)
CELEBREX
CELECOXIB (Celebrex)
CELEXA
CEPHALEXIN (Keflex)
CETIRIZINE (Zyrtec)
CHOLCRYS
CIALIS
CIMETIDINE (Tagamet)
CIPRO
CIPROFLOXACIN (Cipro)
CITALOPRAM (Celexa)
CLARITHROMYCIN (Biaxin)
CLARITIN
CLEOCIN
CLINDAMYCIN (Cleocin)
CLONAZEPAM (Klonopin)
CLONIDINE (Catapres)
CLOPIDOGREL (Plavix)
CODEINE
CODEINE

COLACE
COLCHICINE (Cholcrys)
CONCERTA
CORDARONE
COREG
CORTEF
COUMADIN
COZAAR
CYCLOBENZAPRINE (Flexeril)
CYCLOSPORINE (Sandimmune)
DANTRIUM
DANTROLENE (Dantrium)
DELTASONE
DEPAKOTE
DETROL
DEXMETHYLPHENIDATE (Focalin)
DIABETA
DIAZEPAM (Valium)
DIFLUCAN
DIGOXIN (Lanoxin)
DIHYDROERGOTAMINE (Migranal)
DILANTIN
DILTIAZEM (Cardizem)
DIOVAN
DIPHENHYDRAMINE (Benadryl)
DIPHENHYDRAMINE (Benadryl)
DIPHENOXYLATE/ATROPINE (Lomotil)
DITROPAN
DIVALPROEX (Depakote)
DOCOSANOL (Abreva)
DOCUSATE SODIUM (Colace)
DONEPEZIL (Aricept)
DORYX
DOXAZOSIN (Cardura)
DOXYCYCLINE (Doryx)

DURAGESIC
ECOTRIN
ELAVIL can elevate your mood.
ELDEPRYL
EMETROL
E-MYCIN
ENALAPRIL (Vasotec)
ENBREL
ENDOCET
ENOXAPARIN (Lovenox)
EPINEPHRINE (EpiPen)
EPIPEN
EPOETIN (Procrit)
ERYTHROMYCIN (E-Mycin)
ESZOPICLONE (Lunesta)
ETANERCEPT (Enbrel)
ETHAMBUTOL (Myambutol)
EXCEDRIN
EZETIMIBE (Zetia)
FAMCICLOVIR (Famvir)
FAMOTIDINE (Pepcid)
FAMVIR
FEBUXOSTAT (Uloric)
FENTANYL (Duragesic)
FEXOFENADINE (Allegra)
FINASTERIDE (Propecia)
FINASTERIDE (Proscar)
FLAGYL
FLEXERIL
FLOMAX
FLUCONAZOLE (Diflucan)
FLUOXETINE (Prozac)
FLUTICASONE/SALMETEROL (Advair)
FOCALIN
FORTAZ

FOSAMAX
FUNGIZONE
FUROSEMIDE (Lasix)
GABAPENTIN (Neurontin)
GABITRIL
GARAMYCIN
GEMFIBROZIL (Lopid)
GENTAMICIN (Garamycin)
GLIPIZIDE (Glucotrol)
 GLUCAGEN
GLUCAGON (GlucaGen)
GLUCOPHAGE
GLUCOTROL
GLYBURIDE (Diabeta)
GUAIFENESIN/DEXTROMETHORPHAN (Robitussin DM)
HALDOL
HALOPERIDOL (Haldol)
HEPARIN
HEPARIN
HUMULIN
HYDROCHLOROTHIAZIDE (Hydrodiuril)
HYDROCODONE/ACETAMINOPHIN (Vicodin)
HYDROCODONE/IBUPROFEN (Vicoprofen)
HYDROCORTISONE (Cortef)
HYDRODIURIL
HYTRIN
IBANDRONATE (Boniva)
IBUPROFEN (Motrin)
IMIPRAMINE (Tofranil)
IMITREX
IMODIUM
INDOCIN
INDOMETHACIN (Indocin)
INFLIXIMAB (Remicade)
INH

INSULIN (Humulin)
IPRATROPIUM (Atrovent)
ISOCARBOXAZID (Marplan)
ISONIAZID (INH)
ISOPTO ATROPINE's
K-DUR
KEFLEX
KEPPRA
KETALAR
KETAMINE (Ketalar)
KETOROLAC (Toradol)
KLONOPIN
LAMICTAL
LAMISIL
LAMOTRIGINE (Lamictal)
LANOXIN
LANSOPRAZOLE (Prevacid)
LASIX
LEVAQUIN
LEVETIRACETAM (Keppra)
LEVITRA
LEVODOPA/CARBIDOPA (Sinemet)
LEVOFLOXACIN (Levaquin)
LEVOTHYROXINE (Synthroid)
LIDOCAINE (Xylocaine)
LIORESAL
LIPITOR
LISINOPRIL (Zestril)
LITHIUM
LITHIUM
LOMOTIL
LOPERAMIDE (Imodium)
LOPID
LOPRESSOR
LORATADINE (Claritin)

LORAZEPAM (Ativan)
LOSARTAN (Cozaar)
LOVENOX
LUNESTA
LYRICA
MAALOX LIQUID
MAGNESIUM HYDROXIDE (Milk of Magnesia)
MANNITOL (Osmitrol)
MARPLAN
MAXIPIME
MECLIZINE (Antivert)
MESALAMINE (Asacol)
METAXOLONE (Skelaxin)
METFORMIN (Glucophage)
METHOTREXATE (Rheumatrex)
METHYLPHENIDATE (Concerta)
METHYLPHENIDATE/ DEXMETHYLPHENIDATE
(Adderall)
METOPROLOL (Lopressor)
METRONIDAZOLE (Flagyl)
MIACALCIN
MIGRANAL
MILK OF MAGNESIA
MIRAPEX
MONTELUKAST (Singulair)
MORPHINE
MORPHINE
MOTRIN
MOXIFLOXACIN (Avelox)
MUCOMYST
MYAMBUTOL
MYCOSTATIN
NALOXONE (Narcan)
NAPROXEN (Aleve)
NARCAN

NARDIL
NEURONTIN
NIFEDIPINE (Procardia)
NITROGLYCERIN
NITROGLYCERIN
NIZATIDINE (Axid)
NORVASC
NOVOCAINE
NYSTATIN (Mycostatin)
OMEPRAZOLE (Prilosec)
ONDANSETRON (Zofran)
OS-CAL
OSELTAMIVIR (Tamiflu)
OSMITROL
OXCARBAZEPINE (Trileptal)
OXYBUTYNIN (Ditropan)
OXYCODONE/ACETAMINOPHEN (Endocet)
PANTOPRAZOLE (Protonix)
PARNATE
PAROXETINE (Paxil)
PAXIL
PEPCID
PEPTO-BISMOL
PHENELZINE (Nardil)
PHENYTOIN (Dilantin)
PHOSPHORATED CARBOHYDRATE (Emetrol)
PIOGLITAZONE (Actos)
PLAVIX
POTASSIUM CHLORIDE (K-Dur)
PRAMIPEXOLE (Mirapex)
PREDNISONE (Deltasone)
PREGABALIN (Lyrica)
PREVACID
PRILOSEC
PROAIR

PROCAINE (Novocaine)
PROCARDIA
PROCRIT
PROPECIA
PROSCAR
PROTONIX
PROPYLTHIOURACIL (PTU)
PROZAC
PSEUDOEPHEDRINE (Sudafed)
PTU
PYRAZINAMIDE (PZA)
PZA
QUINAPRIL (Accupril)
RAMELTEON (Rozerem)
Ramipril (Altace)
RANITIDINE (Zantac)
REBEPRAZOLE (Aciphex)
RELENZA
REMICADE
RESTORIL
RETROVIR
RHEUMATREX
RIFADIN
RIFAMPIN (Rifadin)
RISPERDAL
RISPERIDONE (Risperdal)
ROBITUSSIN DM
ROCEPHIN
ROLAIDS
ROSIGLITAZONE (Avandia)
ROZEREM
SANDIMMUNE
SCOPOLAMINE (Transderm-Scop)
SECOBARBITAL (Seconal)
SECONAL

SELEGILINE (Eldepryl)
SERTRALINE (Zoloft)
SILDENAFIL (Viagra)
SIMVASTATIN (Zocor)
SINEMET
SINGULAIR
SKELAXIN
SMZ/TMP
SPIRONOLACTONE (Aldactone)
STRATTERA
SUDAFED
SULFAMETHOXAZOLE/TRIMETHOPRIM (SMZ-TMP)
SUMATRIPTAN (Imitrex)
SYNTHROID
TADALAFIL (Cialis)
TAGAMET
TAMIFLU
TAMSULOSIN
TEGRETOL
TEMAZEPAM (Restoril)
TENORMIN
TERAZOSIN (Hytrin)
TERBINAFINE (Lamisil)
TERBUTALINE (Brethaire)
TIAGABINE (Gabitril)
TOFRANIL
TOLTERODINE (Detrol)
TOPAMAX
TOPIRAMATE (Topamax)
TRAMADOL (Ultram)
TRANSDERM-SCOP
TRANYLCYPROMINE (Parnate)
TRIAMCINOLONE (Azmacort)
TRILEPTAL
TUMS

TYLENOL
ULORIC
ULTRAM
URECHOLINE
VALACYCLOVIR (Valtrex)
VALIUM
VALSARTAN (Diovan)
VALTREX
VANCOCIN
VANCOMYCIN (Vancocin)
VARDENAFIL (Levitra)
VASOTEC
VERAPAMIL (Calan)
VIAGRA
VICODIN
VICOPROFEN
WARFARIN (Coumadin)
XANAX
XYLOCAINE
ZANAMIVIR (Relenza)
ZANTAC
ZESTRIL
ZETIA
ZIDOVUDINE (Retrovir)
ZITHROMAX
ZOCOR
ZOFRAN
ZOLOFT
ZOLPIDEM (Ambien)
ZOVIRAX
ZYLOPRIM
ZYRTEC

Acknowledgements

Special thanks to Marc Dickinson M.F.A. at Des Moines Area Community College and Dr. Steve Pett at Iowa State University for helping me articulate my thoughts as a parent, pharmacist, and teacher through their poetry classes.

My students below who contributed parts or all of certain drug mnemonics and Stephanie Bruner for her editorial work.

Andrea Corns, Toradol
Felisha Montero, -sartan/-pril
Ginger Cochran, Marplan
Karin Hanson, verapamil, methotrexate
Kristine Newton, -sartan/–pril, -olol, beta blockers, alprazolam
Mickenzie Block, spironolactone
Samantha Studer, isocarboxazid
Tracy Thompson, lisinopril

About the author

Tony Guerra graduated with his Doctor of Pharmacy from the University of Maryland in Baltimore, Maryland, and has been a practicing pharmacist for 15 years. He now lives in Ankeny, Iowa, with his wife and triplet daughters Brielle, Rianne, and Teagan. He teaches at Des Moines Area Community College as a chair and instructor of the pharmacy technician program and also teaches health science anatomy and organic and biochemistry. His poetry has been featured in "Expressions" and "Sketch" student literary magazines.

Notes:

Notes:

Notes:

Notes:

Notes:

Notes: